EIGHTY KILOS
OF
SHAME

EIGHTY KILOS OF SHAME

The process of losing the emotional weight

Mart-Mari Breedt

Mart-Mari Breedt • Johannesburg, South Africa

Copyright © 2021 Mart-Mari Breedt
All rights reserved

Cover photos:
Lars Knudsen, Theo Denysschen, Jackie van der Berg

In order to lose weight and maintain it, you have to truly believe that you are worth it.

Eating well and exercising are both acts of self love.

After writing an entire book in my second language, please allow me to write these dedications in my first language.

Vir Derik:
Ek is ongelooflik baie lief vir jou. Dankie dat jy elke dag saam met my 11 maak.

Vir Erik, Lia, Nardus en Adri:
Julle is elkeen baie spesiaal, talentvol en gaan groot dinge in hierdie lewe bereik. Julle is my alles. Ek is baie trots op en lief vir julle elkeen.

I've had it in and then out and then in again tens of times already, but ultimately I've decided to leave out the first names of crucial role players in my story. It is not a case of them not wanting to be named; I did get permission from both my husband and therapist to use their names. Instead, it is a case of me not getting permission from those who had already passed away, like my mother, father, and sister, and I do not wish to use false names for them. Out of respect, I've decided instead to omit the first names of all the vital role players where I could, and it made sense to do that.

Preface

Cold and hard.

No, I am not cold and hard. I am warm and empathetic. Yet, on that Friday afternoon, when my husband pulled me aside to share with me the news of my younger sister's suicide, I didn't feel warm and empathetic.

I went into survival mode right from the start. For me, that meant just thinking of the next logical thing to do, not coming to rest, or taking a moment to absorb the news. Another mum was about to drop my eldest son off from swimming; I needed to be on the alert and listen for her call when she would be at our gate. I had to get my youngest ready for her school concert; I had just more than an hour to do that. I would also have to phone my older sister to share the news with her.

My older sister was in tears; I thought that was so strange. That should have been me! I was the one just eighteen months older — the supposedly closer one. I should have been the one in tears, but I was not. Perhaps I felt a tad jealous because my sister seemed to mourn so effortlessly? My survival and coping mode were too strong, and my anger far too great. I thought that I was supposed to feel grief — that was not what I felt.

I was already deep into my journey to lose my excess eighty kilograms when my sister committed suicide. She was also obese, carrying an additional ninety kilograms with her where ever she used to go. Her inability to control her weight was a significant reason for her desire not to live anymore. I tried to pull her in throughout my weight loss journey — I never could. I thought I could somehow have prevented her suicide. Now I understand that I would not have been able to stop it as she was never open to my message. Yet, at that stage, while learning about her death, the feelings of guilt enveloped me instantly.

The months following her death left me yearning to assist those who were open to my message. It was an internal desire born out of my consistent inability to help my sister. That desire made me say yes to more open meeting talks and produced my online videos, blog, and this book.

I have never seen myself as a writer. I was reluctant to start journaling. Yet, once I realised the benefits of pouring my heart out on paper, I was unable to stop. A few blog posts in a new friend, who had stumbled across my page and blog and reached out to me, planted a seed in my head that made me think that perhaps I did have a book in me. At the very least, I wanted to try.

On the first day, I started writing this book, I already had writer's block! I had no idea how to start, no clue what I was doing, and was way out of my comfort zone. Typically, I am only at my desk in the mornings for job commitments. It is rare for me to be online in the afternoon or early evening. The afternoon that I decided to start writing this book, a colleague noticed I was online and messaged me to inquire about this rare phenomenon out of curiosity. I messaged back explaining my case of writer's block, and he thought it was hilarious. Something extraordinary that happened over the months of writing was my colleagues checking in on my progress and supporting me whenever they saw me online at odd times.

On that first day, while contemplating my writer's block, I realised I would need to approach this book in the same way I approach my blog. I would have to run the chapters out of me. Running the words out of me became my writing process: I would run in the mornings, allowing the inspiration to come to me, and then write in the late afternoon or early evening. Chapter after chapter, or rather, kilometre after kilometre, this book started forming.

This book is the sum of hurt, desperation, and love, mauled into shape by hundreds of kilometres of running on the tarmac.

May it be an inspiration to whoever lay their eyes on it.

Introduction

I am probably the most ordinary person you will ever meet. I am a wife and a mum of four beautiful children, two boys and two girls, and one angel in heaven. After my run each morning, I spend the first half of my day working a typical office job. After lunch, I fetch my children from school and then play mum's taxi across Johannesburg's northern suburbs. I am average looking, rather tall, and currently weighing a "normal" weight, meaning I am not fat, nor am I skinny.

Yes, I see myself as very ordinary. I just happened to do something extraordinary: over two years and ten months, I had managed to lose just over eighty kilograms of weight. I had no surgery to lose this weight. I also used no supplements, tablets, or any other form of "magic potion". I also had no personal trainer or drill sergeant. I merely ate healthily, and I exercised using my discretion. I still do those two things.

I can think of only one thing that I do, that others perhaps do less: I question everything. I ponder, I brew, and I meditate. I never take anything at face value. As far as I can remember, I have always been like this; only previously, I used to keep my thoughts to myself. Now I share my thoughts and my hurt, hoping that others will find it relatable. I desire that my story inspire others to perform introspection and face their demons.

My childhood years were not easy. I observe that a lot of adults blame their problems on their childhood. Perhaps they are correct, and our childhoods are to blame for many of our adult troubles? I am in no denial that my childhood was a luxury compared to those who had issues way more complicated than I ever did. But I have had my share of pain. Emotional hurt was part of my life for as long as I can remember. I have misjudged the amount of hurt I've experienced for many, many years, believing that my hurt was neither significant nor of importance. When I meet up with people requiring my insights into their weight problems and hear testimonies of their experiences, I often feel that my hurt cannot compare to what they have encountered and that they should not even be talking to me. I have even labelled my pain as being ordinary.

Someone entered my rather average life and made me discover or rediscover the pain that I was carrying. This pain prevented me from living life to the fullest and was a big reason I struggled and had always found it very hard to maintain my weight.

I once explained my healing process using a metaphor. I saw myself making a beautiful, smooth and rich butterscotch sauce. I needed to melt down some hard boiled butterscotch sweets for this sauce, those that come individually wrapped. However, before adding the sweets, I neglected to remove the wrappers. When I introduced the wrapped candies to my sauce, it became a clumpy and inedible mess. The wrappers caused none of the sweets to become incorporated.

I have kept the complex and problematic parts of my life hidden or wrapped up for years. Some of those parts I hid so well that I struggled to take myself back to them. I needed someone to help me unwrap and then teach me how to deal with these problems. I never realised that I needed this person in my life. These difficult times are a part of my life that I cannot wish away regardless of how much I want. I needed to address them, even though I didn't want to. I wanted to become that beautiful, rich sauce, not remain the mess I was.

Weigh-Less
Goal Weight Membership Award

This is to certify that

Mart-Mari Breedt

Achieved

Goal Weight Membership

On 10 December 2019

Having lost a total of 80.2 kgs

Mary

Mary Holroyd
(Founder and Chairman of the Weigh-Less Organisation)

Group Leader

I Am A Quitter

I am a quitter. By telling you that I am a serial yo-yo dieter, I tell you that I am a quitter. That is who I am and who I had always been. Probably also who I will return to eventually as well. I have an all or nothing attitude to life. I start something with the best intentions, and when things don't go the way I want them to go, I quit and revert to who I was. I can do this in the blink of an eye. And because I am so head-strong, few things can get me out of a slump when I'd convinced myself that that is where I belong and have always belonged.

"Anything worth doing is worth doing well."

"I don't start anything if I cannot see myself being successful at it."

"I will give my very best to make a success of something."

"Things are not working out like I'd like them to work out. My best wasn't good enough. I'll rather just quit and crawl back to where I came from."

These are my own words. These are the things I tell myself at night when I cannot sleep.

* * *

28 March 2021

Today I am sitting here in despair. I took a chance at writing a book. I wanted to be successful at it. In my heart, I knew that I was not a writer. On the recommendation of a friend, I started something that I couldn't see myself seeing through successfully. Now things are not going how I'd like them to go, and I want to quit.

For the past almost four months, I had been writing. Pouring my heart out onto paper and enjoying it, finding my release. I posted some of my writings on my blog and had good feedback. Receiving good feedback gave me hope. Some of my chapters I shared with friends and also received good feedback. That also gave me hope that I was doing the right thing and heading in the right direction. This past week, I worked with another writer to complete an initial grammar and punctuation edit. It was going well. I felt that I was almost done with my book and was keen on submitting it for publishing. When accepted for publishing, I know that there would still be many more professional edits that would need to happen. I was not put off by that prospect; I just wanted to get to the point of my book being accepted for publishing first — one hurdle at a time.

Last night the other writer helping me told me that she feels that my book was nowhere near ready for publishing yet. She believed that significant parts of the book would need to be re-written. She also felt parts were still missing. I appreciate her honesty immensely, as the only feedback I'd gotten up to last night had been positive. But now I feel like everyone has been lying to me and was laughing behind my back. I know that is not true, but I cannot help feeling like it is.

I am not a writer. I had always said that I am not a writer! I want to quit and not write anymore. I do not have a book in me. Why didn't anyone stop me when I started? I started journaling for myself. I wanted a way to get my feelings worded and out. Why did I ever decide to share that which I'd written? I should not have done that. I was a fool to try and help others through my story. Why did no one tell me that my work was shit? These are the words that keep going round and round in my head now.

One of the parts this other writer felt was missing is an in-depth description of the obese person I used to be. I had been dieting for such a long time. I had been at goal weight for a while now as well. I had been presenting my talks, writing my book and working myself so far away from the person I'd used to be that I had forgotten who that person was. I cannot see myself writing an entire chapter on the person I used to be.

Last night while I was lying in bed thinking about my crap book and my dumb dreams, I realised that the person I used to be, has not completely disappeared yet. The person I used to be is the same person currently thinking of quitting her book and wanting to make a silent disappearance of the face of the earth. I do not want to be that person anymore. I thought that I had put her behind me, but she comes out when I feel that I have reached the point where I cannot go on anymore.

* * *

The obese me was a hopeless and pathetic quitter. I would follow a diet religiously or binge until I felt that I could burst. There was no in-between, no logic, no half-measures.

I knew that I was obese. I knew that I needed to do something about it, but I preferred always taking the easy way out and remaining the way I was. I couldn't see myself not having an entire slab of chocolate or not eating all of the children's leftovers after I had an already large meal. I'd used to order from a menu by selecting the food I thought would be the most.

I would postpone starting a diet if I saw an advertisement for a new type of chocolate or flavour of chips, thinking that my life would somehow be incomplete if I didn't have the opportunity to at least try this new thing first. I saw food as adding value to my life. I loved food. I lived to eat. I saw going on a diet as temporary suffering that I would need to endure for a while until I could get to a point where I could safely eat "normally" again.

I would lay out a spread so massive for my children's parties that we should've had leftover treats for weeks. I somehow managed to finish all the leftover treats the day after the party. And if asked about it, I would say that they would've spoiled if I didn't eat them. I never drank water. I drank litres of soft drinks every day. We had to have it in our fridge. If there weren't a soft drink, I would drink glasses full of milk. At parties, I used to stand by the food all the time. I could eat all the food for the party by myself. Buffet restaurants used to be my favourite type of restaurant as I could then eat as much as I'd like. I piled it on, plate after plate after plate.

What I ate and how I looked was nothing compared to the horror of the person I was. I used to feel entitled to people not judging me. If it only appeared that someone else was thinking that I did not look good, I'd get angry and upset and start pitying myself. I was angry and sad all the time and believed that it was everyone around me's fault. I was never to blame. I had no confidence, and I was overly emotional and sensitive. When someone dared to tell me that I should try to lose weight, I would give them every excuse I could think of as to why I couldn't do it, along with an explanation of all my previous failed attempts. Nobody could suggest a solution to me that I didn't feel myself to be already an expert at failing.

The only thing I thought that I was good at was that I was clever. I am good at maths, logical thinking and problem-solving. I built my entire self-esteem around my ability to solve complex problems and being intelligent. I expected people to respect me because of my intellect. Ironically, I could not solve the biggest problem I had, which was my weight.

I had no drive to better myself or to grow as a person. I felt there was no hope for me and that I was doomed to be fat forever. I proved this repeatedly by losing weight and then regaining it again. See? I told you I could not do it! Do you believe me now? Are you happy now? I could not see a way out of my situation.

And here I sit now, thinking again that I cannot do it. I start raking up the excuses: I am not a writer, I have never been a writer, I write in my second language, writing is not my destiny, I should leave the writing to the people who know how to write.

When I look in the mirror, all I see is the obese Mart-Mari looking back at me.

Peering Through The *Jakkals Draad*

We were still staying in the only home I'd known up to then. The home I grew up in and stayed in for most of my primary school years. It was a mining house. We could stay in this house because of a housing benefit included in my father's income package. When my dad retired, that benefit fell away. My parents rented this house for a few years after that, considered purchasing it, but then decided against buying it later.

This house was a corner house with a massive garden and sidewalk. A vast garden was always appealing to my mum as she was a passionate and talented gardener. I have not inherited her green fingers. This house had *Jakkals draad*, diamond chain link fencing, as a fence. My mum tried to add some privacy by planting runner-plants and other climbers all along the *Jakkals draad*. Rustenburg was dry and warm; my mum's attempts at covering our wire fence mainly were futile.

It was late in the afternoon, the sun had already started setting, and I was sitting cross-legged and peering through the *Jakkals draad*. I could see the lights going on in some of our neighbours' houses. Perhaps our lights were also on? I couldn't know if they were as I was sitting with my back facing our house. I was looking out towards the street.

The spot I was sitting in was dry and dusty and under the Frangipani closest to our gate. Our gate, also constructed out of chain link fencing, was open — as it mostly was. That was the way things were then. Gates were left unlocked and mostly widely flung open unless you were not home. Our neighbours across the street from us didn't even have a fence or gate. I could've walked out of the gate, but I didn't. I was sitting in the dust, under the Frangipani, watching the sun setting and the street lights and other house lights coming on.

That Frangipani was one of my favourite places to play. Frangipanis do not have a lot of foliage, and a big one, like that one, was a lovely jungle gym and resting place. I could've found a spot for myself in that Frangipani. Then I would've been off the ground. But that seemed like a fun thing to do. I was not there to play, so I was sitting in the dust — planning, thinking, strategising.

I was locked out of our house — kicked out — forbidden to go back in. My mum was still screaming inside; I could hear her. She was not shouting at me anymore; she was yelling at my dad. I didn't hear my dad. My dad never raised his voice. I did not hear my dad, but I could still recall what my mum had said to me moments before. I was saying it to myself over and over.

"Get out! I never want to see you again!"

"I don't care what happens to you. I want you out of my house. You don't belong here. You shouldn't be here. I don't want you here. I want you gone!"

"No, you cannot take anything with you. Everything is mine. Everything belongs to me. You have nothing. You are nothing. Get out! Go!"

My left arm was still hurting from where my mum had repeatedly smacked me. My right arm was also not feeling well from when my mum grabbed hold of it to drag me and flung me out. She threw me out of the door onto our slate *stoep*. Then she forcefully slammed and locked the door.

I cannot even remember why my mum was mad at me. I must've done something terrible.

Sitting there in the dust, under the Frangipani, I was scared, crying, and unsure what to do next. I wiped my tears with the back of my dust-covered hand, creating a mess in the process. The more I messed, the more I cried. Ultimately smeared-off streaks of mud covered the entire front of my nightdress. Why does my mum hate me so much? Eventually, I cried myself to sleep.

I know we all have two parents and that my dad could've stood up for me a million times. But he didn't — he always took my mum's side.

My mum was the love of his life, as I suppose it should be. He never shouted at me or hit me, though, and he usually tried to correct what went wrong, even if it was only afterwards when he had a break of my mum's directed anger himself, in my eyes, that made him my hero. My dad suffered from the same problem: the desire to please others coupled with the belief that he had to earn love.

I am not sure how late in the evening it was when my dad came to wake me up and fetch me; it was already very dark by then. By that time, my mum was already asleep herself.

Myself And Others

We had many trees on our Grade One playground, which enabled us to play a simple game. There needed to be one fewer tree than the number of children playing. Every child would stand next to a tree, and one child would be "on". Whenever the "on" child called out "Skoert!", everyone had to race to a new tree. The person not standing by a tree was "on" for the next round.

"Do you want to play with us?" one of my Grade One classmates invited me.

"Yes! I'd love to play," I replied immediately and probably over eagerly. I wanted the others to include me.

Playing the game was not as much fun as I thought it would be. I did not feel included. I felt singled out. Because I was so overweight, I could not run very fast. Because I couldn't run very fast, I was always "on", and the other children began teasing me and luring me out. I was close to tears, but I didn't want them to see the effect they were having on me.

The following day during break time, I was invited again: "Do you want to play with us?".

Yes! Yes, I want to. I do not want to sit by myself. I asked, "Are you going to be playing the same game as yesterday?"

"Yes, we are."

"Okay. I will rather sit here and watch you guys play," I replied.

A month or two into Grade One, we received notice of netball practices starting. I wanted to play netball, but the other girls were fitter and leaner than I was. Still, I asked my dad to take me, and I reported for practice.

It was just a regular practice — the first practice of the season. We were Grade Ones — we were all novices. Our coach had us throw some hoops and pass the ball around. At the end of the session, our coach told me that I did not need to come to practise again. I did not make the team. I didn't even realise we were trying out for teams! That was the first and last time I ever raised my hand to try out for any sport. Afterwards, my mum said it was just as well; my dad wouldn't have been able to keep up with taking me to practices anyway.

I was never a big fan of being active. During our activity period, our teacher had us climb across the monkey bars one day. I could not manage it. I could not manage to let go with one hand while hanging by my other hand and at the same time reaching across to grab the next bar. I started crying. Our teacher tried helping me, but I was scared, and I tried placing my legs around her for stability; instead, I smeared mud caked under my shoes all around the top of her dress. Afterwards, in class, she scolded me in front of the entire class because I made a mess of her dress. I did not know what to say, so I just looked down and avoided her gaze. I loved my teacher; I felt so bad for making a mess of her beautiful dress. I felt ashamed of struggling to climb across the monkey bars. I did not want to partake in our activity periods anymore. I started making excuses not to attend them and would often "forget" my activity clothes at home on purpose. That excuse of not bringing my activity clothes failed most of the time as the teacher would have me join in then while wearing my school uniform. For years this continued until I started menstruating and stained underwear or sanitary towels underneath my dress made me not suitable to join in during the activity period in school uniform anymore.

Reading opened up an entire world that didn't require me to have any friends or be active. When I figured out the hang of reading, which was around the middle of Grade One, I submerged myself into the world of books. I used to read whatever I could find. Every break time and in the afternoons after finishing my school work, you would find me with my nose in a book. Nothing books couldn't teach me, and I became independent of anyone else to gain knowledge. When the Grade Ones were allowed in the school library during break times, I'd sit there and read. Sitting in the library felt better than sitting outside alone. I was not proud of my friendless situation and didn't want the other children to see me sitting by myself.

It was in Grade Three that we first started writing tests. My first graded test, a spelling test, received a grade of six marks out of a possible ten. I still remember it so well. I went home that afternoon and asked my dad if six out of ten was a good mark. I had no idea that it was a terrible mark. If I knew, I would've kept quiet about it as my mum reprimanded me for bringing home such a poor grade. I vowed never to bring home such a poor grade ever again — and I didn't; I worked tirelessly to become and remain a straight-A student. I was consistently at the top, primarily first, of my class year after year after year. I brought home so many trophies, book prices and other awards. But none of my achievements I could trade in for love or friendship. I believed that I could earn love, and I spent my entire life trying to deserve it. I never could. Instead, I was labelled the overweight loner with her nose stuck in a book. My awards couldn't even make me love myself.

When I tell the story of being a loner to my eldest daughter now, she reckons that I was wise not to sit with other girls' groups. She says that there is constant bickering in these groups and that often she is expected to pick sides in arguments not involving her. She wants peace and some friendly faces to talk to over break time. I can understand her perspective, but I am so proud of her for sticking it out with her friends and not hiding away in a corner somewhere like I did, hoping that no one would see her.

Being a loner continued throughout my school career. I was fortunate to have an excellent and committed debating partner in high school from Grade Eight, but that was about the only meaningful and closest relationship to a friendship. However, my final school year was peculiar as I was elected to be part of the school's student leadership body. Years of constantly achieving the highest grade in my class caused some popularity — enough popularity to see me elected. I could not spend each break time in the library anymore, I now had some leadership duties to perform, and I had another member who would work with me each time. And I somehow and suddenly had a boyfriend as well. For someone who spent eleven of her twelve school years not fitting in anywhere, to suddenly belong to a formal body of people, it felt surreal. I did not know what to make of all the attention. But I knew that I did not want to lose it.

Being starved of friendship for many years, whenever I find myself in a friendly relationship, I try to protect it — often to my disadvantage. I resent it when I lose a friend. I know people move on or grow apart, but it is a brutal reality for me to accept. I give a lot of myself in a relationship, and I enjoy being able to help others. Perhaps years of silently observing people from the top of a book had given me a better understanding of relationship dynamics? I do find myself able to tune in to and connect with others quickly. I am an open-hearted person.

This book contains a lot about my therapy journey. My therapy journey only started after losing my eighty kilograms and reaching my goal weight. Before therapy commenced, I already had an assignment handed to me as preparation for our first session. The task was to go back into my child mode and draw a self-portrait, and then everything I felt guilty or shameful about around this portrait — even if that guilt or shame was placed on me by others. I labelled this drawing my self-and-shame-portrait.

I could draw a lot of shame, but the self-portrait part of my self-and-shame-portrait was not apparent. I was doubtful about how I should depict myself. Certain things were clear: I should sketch long hair, a round face and an overweight body. But at what age? And what should this child be doing? What was the vision that popped into my head when I thought of myself as a child? I ended up drawing an overweight girl, with long hair, in a school uniform, sitting by herself, reading a book during break time. That felt like the most accurate depiction of myself as a child. And as an adult, I can sometimes still see myself in that image.

Eighty Kilos of Shame

My Fat Trap

The objective of the game was to go as fast as you could. But I could barely fit into the seat of the go-kart and even less go as fast as I could. As my weight weighed down the kart, I became the slowest team member and lost valuable ground when the other teams' drivers overtook me repeatedly. The rest of my squad feared my turn to drive next. One of the team-building purposes is identifying weak points and working around them. Right? I wanted to continue driving, but I also wanted our team to do well. So as a team player, I relinquished my spot and asked one of our faster team members to drive in my place.

I felt trapped in fat for almost my entire life — literally buried within a mountain of fat.

I couldn't move freely.
I couldn't fully be who I wanted to be.
I couldn't do what I wanted to do.
I couldn't wear what I wanted to wear.
My health was suffering due to my excess weight.

There was no quick escape from my fat trap — not even a way to put the weight aside temporarily. And I did it all to myself. I was trapped in my mountain of fat but allowed to observe others who seemingly had it all figured out and were free to live the lives they wanted to live.

Not only was I observing others, but they were also observing me. How could they not? I stood out! I was a huge, tall mountain of a woman weighing one-hundred-and-sixty-five kilograms at my heaviest. I felt most judged by strangers and those who never took the time to know me.

I always went to our varsity socials; I had never been someone that would not show up. Yet during these socials, I would always spend the entire evening as a wallflower. No one would ask me to dance or even look in my direction. I wasn't even looking for a boyfriend, I already had one, but no one cared or took an interest in me. Were the other girls really that more interesting than me? Perhaps not, but it must've appeared that way, or I was just too ugly to be considered good company.

During our varsity residence first-year dinner, I received an award for our group's best academic achievement of the year. Later that evening, I overheard some girls saying how surprised they were as they always thought I was stupid. They had never taken the time to get to know me. They could only make that judgement based on my physical appearance.

One day, I was walking and approached by a homeless person who begged for coins. I refrain from carrying any cash with me, and when I told him that I did not have any money on me, he started verbally abusing me by pointing my weight out to me and that I must have something on me as I probably bought food everywhere I went. He added that I probably spend my days lying on a couch, watching TV and eating. I understand that he was hungry and frustrated, but he was also saying aloud what many other strangers were probably thinking.

In my experience, strangers judge obese people as lazy, dumb and uninteresting. One of my proofreaders pointed out that being jolly is another common observation of obese people. I can see how that can be the case, but I've never experienced someone seeing me as jolly with my thoughtful and solemn persona. I would usually be the last person invited to any social gathering.

I wanted to be thin. I earnestly did. But I could not find a solution to my problem. Finding my way through and out of my mountain of fat felt like navigating an extremely complicated maze. Every twist, corner and turn promised a new way out. Neither I nor anyone else had an aerial view of this maze to help me navigate it.

I have tried so many possible ways to navigate my maze. When you want to lose weight, the only answer is to start a diet. The problem is that the diet industry is massive, and the number of diet and lifestyle options on offer is overwhelming. Every diet has its own wonderful, unbelievable success stories. Advertisements to get the word out to our ears. Terrible before photos and beautiful after photos. Promises of success that made me feel even more like a failure.

My first diet was a starvation diet. I tried out the 'calories in' must be less than 'calories out' theory. It works; it genuinely does work. But it is not sustainable. I tried it because it was the most straightforward and cheapest option, but as soon as life became too much for me, I quitted and promptly gained back all my weight again.

I had also eaten according to my blood type. My blood type is A-positive, and according to the prescripts for an A-positive diet, my diet is supposed to be primarily vegetarian. I am not supposed to eat red meat, dairy, wheat or drink wine etc. I have never found any diet that excludes something, like my blood type, a banting or a no-fat diet, to work for me. When I have to avoid eating something, I find that the cravings become unbearable. A diet is supposed to be sustainable. How am I supposed to follow a diet for life when I cannot even follow it for a few days?

I have walked the aisles in the pharmacy, browsing for magic potions to help me lose weight. I've sat for hours mesmerised by infomercials of a new type of shake, diet or exercise gimmick. I've tried drugs to suppress my appetite or make my metabolism faster. I've used meal replacement shakes, and I've taken tablets to make food pass through my intestinal tract more quickly. I've taken water retention tablets, and I've tried various types of fat burning medicine. The worst I've ever felt was taking metabolism-enhancing drugs. The drugs chased my heart rate up so much that I could constantly hear it from inside my ears.

Weaving my way through the overwhelming variety of available diets and choosing one was already complicated enough. But my struggle never ended when I decided on a new diet, product, lifestyle or gimmick. I then had to stick with that choice, lose the weight and see it through. Seems obvious, right? But for me, that was more difficult than choosing something in the first place! I can best describe the process as being the tiny marble in the marble maze, constantly rolling back or taking a wrong turn, never finding the hollow space where I could finally come to rest.

I am a software engineer. In Computer Science, we call these problems NP-C (Non-polynomial Complete) problems. In layman's terms, this means that once you have a solution to the problem, it is easy to verify that it is a solution. Someone who has already lost their excess weight can easily say, "Yes, this worked for me. Here, this is how I did it."

While verifying a solution is easy, there is no quick way to determine a solution in the first place. The solution space is too broad. I.e. there is no way to exhaustively search through all permutations of various potential solutions using polynomial algorithms. The best solution to an NP-C problem is to use heuristics or approximation. But losing weight is not a mathematical problem; I could never use mathematical algorithms to approximate my way out of my problem.

I used to dream of reaching my goal weight. I saw my goal weight as this magical place where I will keep the weight off forever. Never has a bigger lie been told. And yet, that is how being thin was sold to me — and is sold to many others. Reaching my goal weight was described as the finishing line. Once I've crossed this finishing line, I will remain on the winning side of it for the rest of my life. But in reality, I was the tiny marble just waiting to be knocked out of its concave resting spot by the next bump in the road. Never able to escape for good. I have always found the diet odds stacked against me.

In December 2019, I found myself at the end of an eighty kilograms weight loss journey, wondering just where I could find some glue to secure this tiny marble. Or wondering if there is perhaps something that I can do to ensure that neither myself nor anyone else bumps or rocks the maze and hits the marble out of its place.

So much information is out there on how to lose weight; it is overwhelming. Yet, there is scant information on maintaining a considerable weight loss. The most popular view on weight loss maintenance is that it is impossible. Once a fattie, always a fattie.

Realising that I cannot rely on solely my strong willpower, but not having had a chance yet to discuss this with Therapist, I started to blog. In my very first blog post, when I still knew nothing, I asked these questions:

"If you are a person of 'normal' weight reading this, I'd like to ask you this: How do thin people stay thin? Do you ever consider your diet? Do you ever weigh yourself? And if you do, how often? I come from an overweight family, and all I've ever known is how to be fat ..."

I have since come to realise that the one group of people, the people I view as never having struggled with their weight and the other group of people, ex-fatties like myself, do not play the same game. I am resting in a hollow space, waiting for life to knock me out again. They are not in a maze at all. The weight loss field is not one they have ever needed to navigate. I started my maintenance journey by asking the wrong questions. Even the right answers to the wrong questions do not mean anything to your problem. Instead, I should have asked:

"How did I get in the maze in the first place?"

The Turning Point

Sunday, 5 February 2017 — my eldest son was swimming at a gala while my husband was at home looking after our other three children. The thing with these galas is that they are just so busy. So many parents. So many swimmers. So little space. I always tried to be there as early as possible to get a seat — in reality, I needed two — otherwise, I would probably end up standing during the entire event. Standing was not something I was particularly keen to do — especially not when weighing more than one-hundred-and-sixty-five kilograms.

For years, my doctor told me that I needed to lose weight. She was not just telling me this for my health in general but more specifically because I needed surgery to repair some abdominal hernias that had been troubling me. It is not that I did not want to lose weight — I didn't like being obese. I didn't want to be obese. Nobody likes being obese. Nobody wants to search for two open spaces next to each other at a gala stadium when it is not for themselves and another person but just because they need those two slots to have even a slight chance of sitting comfortably. Nobody enjoys sore, swollen ankles with skin stretched so much that it becomes dry and itchy — making you bloody miserable. Nobody wants to miss their son's winning touch in the pool because they couldn't stand up fast enough to see over the head of the parent in front of them who had suddenly jumped up.

The unfortunate reality of obesity is this. You can always take a break from a busy schedule, a hectic work routine, or a crazy household timetable; you can go on holiday for a week or two, but you cannot take a break from being obese. It is not the type of thing you can park for two weeks and say, "Right, for the next two weeks, I am going to leave my fat suit at home and be thin." It just doesn't work that way. It is a constant battle, a constant source of stress.

My children's school has a school mascot. When I see the mascot, I never know who is inside the suit until I get close enough to talk to them. When you are obese, you carry your fat suit costume with you wherever you go. You cannot hide your identity in your fat suit hoping that no one will know who it is. Everyone knows it's you! You have nowhere to hide; if anything, you stick out like a sore thumb. You can still sometimes hide other problems, such as financial or marital problems, but your weight problem is not a secret that you can hide. You carry the shame of your excess weight with you wherever you go.

About a decade ago, I read a story about an upset husband's outburst at his overweight wife. He told her that he could not understand why she could not lose weight. In his mind, dieting was simple maths, 'calories in' should be fewer than 'calories out'.

Having spent most of my life as a morbidly obese person, stories like these pull at my heartstrings. Not that my husband ever said that to me. If there were a picture in the dictionary next to "Unconditional love", it would be a photo of my husband. He never told me that I needed to lose weight. On the contrary, he always told me how beautiful I was and how much he loved me. All four of our children were born during my very overweight years. He supported me whenever I wanted to try a new diet and when I desired to stop and not continue dieting anymore. He made me feel beautiful and loved even when the rest of the world was anything but loving and kind.

Stories like these upset me because they feed the stereotype of overweight people perceived as dumb and lazy. Why can fat people not figure it out? If it is as simple an equation as 'calories in' should be fewer than 'calories out', why is obesity such a significant problem?

On that particular Sunday, I was feeling the enormity of this question. Why could I not just figure out how to lose weight? I was a serial yo-yo dieter. Whenever I lost some weight, I would always regain it — with interest — and I was the first to jest while crying on the inside: weight loss must be one of the best interest rates going.

In my yo-yo diet history, I was the most successful at losing weight when I tried Weigh-Less for the first time before my second child's birth. I lost weight even while pregnant with my daughter but regained everything back after her birth. I couldn't bring myself to go back to our group meetings initially because I had a difficult birth and suffered post-natal depression. The longer I stayed away, the easier it became not to go. After a short while, I was so far down the rabbit hole again that I felt ashamed to go back.

Weigh-Less is different from other commercial eating programs as it offers a support structure in the form of your Weigh-Less group and group leader. I am not a person who likes to admit that I need help. I like accepting assistance even less. As far as possible, I try to help myself as I do not wish to be needy. I see requiring other people's support as a sign of weakness. Joining Weigh-Less for the first time was already hard for me. I was not too fond of the fact that I couldn't figure out how to lose weight by myself.

My group leader at the time invested a great deal of her time and energy in assisting me on my weight loss journey. I received fantastic support from the group as well. Everyone was excited about my daughter's birth and wanted to see how I progressed after her birth. But I failed everyone, including, and especially, myself. I gained a great deal more weight than just the weight I lost at the time. I didn't have it in me to go back and admit defeat. I was too proud.

So I'd been trying to lose the weight that I needed to before I would be allowed to have surgery, but this time I was doing it independently. I tried meal replacement shakes, papaya tablets, various fat burning, and metabolism-enhancing concoctions. Nothing seemed to work. Any weight I did lose would soon be back, but not without bringing a few friends along. I was doomed to be fat forever! Dumb and lazy and not able to figure it out. I am a hardworking person. I am an employee, a wife, and a mother of four children. I am also not dumb. But what other conclusion could people who had watched me over many years flick-flacking my way through weight loss and weight gain make? I felt ashamed of my inability to lose weight.

On that particular Sunday, I was also having difficulty with hernias.

A section of my small intestine felt trapped, and I constantly tried to push it back, but it just kept popping out again. It was so painful.

A friend of mine, who was also overweight herself, was sitting next to me. She could see that I wasn't feeling well. It was warm and humid by the pool. I could feel the sweat pooling at the back of my knees and in between my thighs. I knew that come evening; I would have to wash and dry the same dress for the next day, as it was the last dress that still fitted me. I kept on holding my stomach. My son was swimming so well, winning medals and ribbons. I should just have been proud and enjoyed his success with him. But I wasn't. I was sore, miserable, and uncomfortable. Deeply unhappy with myself, I could not even be happy for him. All I wanted was to be a good mum interested in her children's lives.

My friend began talking about a new diet that she had started. She suggested that I join her, and then the two of us could support each other. I was hardly listening. I felt I didn't have it in me to start a new dieting project and hope for 'a new hope'. I needed to start doing something that I knew worked. I did need support, my friend was correct in that, but I needed assistance from someone who had already walked the weight loss journey herself.

There is a lot that I could not do as an obese person. I couldn't tie my shoes. I couldn't sit on just any chair. I could not fly unless I were willing to buy two tickets. Certain cars were out of the question, as I could not fit in them. Wiping my bum from the back was not possible. There was so much I couldn't do, but I could still make a phone call. I needed to swallow my pride and contact my previous group leader. I reached her the very same day.

I always say that on that Sunday afternoon, three miracles happened:

I had enough life-saving self-esteem and love for myself left to swallow my pride and contact my previous group leader.

My previous group leader had the same phone number after more than seven years — luckily. The week that I re-joined was also the week she resigned as a group leader. She intended to do missionary work in Africa.

My previous group leader remembered me and was still facilitating a Weigh-Less group just a stone's throw away from our house, and it was at a time that I could attend.

Just two days later, I walked into my previous group leader's group again and learnt that I had more than eighty kilograms to lose. I had no idea how much weight I needed to lose before then, as my home bathroom scale's maximum weight limit is one-hundred-and-thirty kilograms. It had been years that I had weighed too much to weigh myself at home. Discovering that I needed to lose eighty kilograms was a massive shock. It was hard to have someone who has already helped me in the past see just how much I had wasted her time by undoing all the hard work and time that she had invested in me. It was hard to face the cold, hard fact that I had lost my way to the extent that I had to 'lose' a whole person — the sheer volume of weight that I needed to lose felt insurmountable.

I had a story developer help me work through my story to find where she felt something was still missing. One of the things she questioned was my description of what it felt like to learn that I have eighty kilograms to lose. She asked: "Explain to me what you felt that first time you learned that you have eighty kilograms to lose. I don't completely grasp the feeling from your current description."

"It felt like an insurmountable task," I replied.

"But what does insurmountable feel like?"

"Impossible. It feels impossible."

"But what does impossible feel like?"

"Impossible feels like going home and eating …"

But I did not go home and eat as if it was my last meal ever on this earth, even though I felt despondent and like stuffing my face with potato chips. Instead, I had to go and tell my husband what a massive task lay ahead of me. That was a complicated thing to do. My husband had just become the husband to a wife who was just more than eighty kilograms overweight.

I knew that he had been that for years perhaps, but having the task measured and verbalised made it so much more real. My husband is the man who was supposed to find me desirable, think I am beautiful, touch me, have sex with me — and then I had to tell him that I have eighty kilograms to lose. Not the greatest of libido boosters, and I am sure not the type of news any wife would like to share with her husband.

Two years and ten months of dieting and focus followed to reach my goal weight.

Later in 2017, our group received a new group leader who continued as the group leader of our group until I received my goal weight certificate. By the end of my first year of following the Weigh-Less program, I had already lost enough weight to be considered for the hernia operation that I needed. Our group leader also asked me to present my first open meeting talk at that stage. At that time, she saw something in me that I was still unaware of myself.

Several times I wondered why I'd been successful this time around. Was it because I had a plan that I worked through methodically? I didn't lose eighty kilograms; I lost eight kilograms ten times. Or was I just primarily motivated as I required surgery insidiously impacting my life? Did all my previous attempts at losing weight call for only additional motivation then? Was extra incentive that which was lacking all along? Why then did I continue and see my weight loss journey through after I had my surgery?

After a great deal of soul-searching, I think the answer has something to do with this: this was the first profound weight loss journey I'd been on since my mother had passed away.

The Fear Of Regaining

The world around me had changed, and I have never been more aware of it.

People die, leaders change, buildings are erected or torn down. Noise, events, buzz — happening all around me. Usually, I, choosing to live without a radio or television, am oblivious. Ignorant?

But not today. Today it is quiet. No noise. Dead silence. Post-apocalyptic-ally eerie quiet. The quietness is out of place. It screams! Like an unruly toddler, it demands my attention.

It is the first Saturday of the lockdown. It is my first time out of the house. It is early morning, and I am driving out to buy groceries. Buying groceries is something I do every single Saturday morning. Except for another vehicle from Martin's funeral home (I kid you not!), the road is deserted.

Am I the only one in Johannesburg doing shopping on a Saturday morning? What are the odds of that happening?

I feel like I am doing something wrong, as if I am somewhere I am not supposed to be. I am an honest, law-abiding woman, and this feeling is making me anxious. Please don't arrest me! Did I miss the memo? Damn this 'no news'-strategy. Whose bright idea was it anyway? I need to buy these groceries. We haven't stockpiled anything and have four children to feed. They need to eat.

Other than the employees, there is no one else at the greengrocer. I am the only customer. Standing almost by myself in the massive store feels so wrong. I chat to the owner, he shows me how well-stocked the shelves are, but I can see he is worried. I buy a little more than I usually would. If it were not for this place, I would never have managed to reach my goal weight. They have supplied me with affordable fresh produce for years. One of the owners was my neighbour from across the street. I desperately need this place to survive the lockdown; otherwise, I will become fat again.

The previous day my husband and I had a huge fight. For the first time, I ran within the perimeters of my garden. Running in such a small space is a silly thing to do, and the silliness of it is reflected on my Garmin app when my running route appears as a childish red squiggle. My husband thought he could cheat the system. He always thinks he is so clever. He ran out of our top gate down the street to our bottom gate — a slightly longer and easier route.

I screamed at him, "Are you crazy? Someone is going to see and report you. Please do not try to find a loophole around the new laws. Do you want them to say that running in your garden is illegal as well? How will I exercise then? If I cannot exercise, I will become fat again."

Fat? The whole world is worried about a virus. And me? I am concerned about becoming fat again.

On the day that I reached my goal weight, I went home and ate the meal that I had set out to prepare for us that evening. The following day I got up and weighed myself, just as I have done almost every morning ever since I've been able to weigh myself on my home scale once again. I weighed out my breakfast and stuck to my eating formula as I have been doing for the previous almost three years.

After a few weeks of doing this, I thought, 'There must be more to goal weight life than this?'

But I did not know how to free myself from dieting. I feared that if I just let myself go, just even a little bit, that I would pick up all eighty kilograms again.

Two of my goals for 2020 were to get to as many Weigh-Less groups as possible to share my story and to focus on and improve my running.

Both goals were aimed at keeping myself accountable, with me being very strict and demanding of myself.

When lockdown hit, I started panicking as I couldn't do my open meeting talks anymore, and road running also became illegal. So I started doing online videos for my fellow Weigh-Less members, including members of the general public, which grew beyond my wildest expectations. I also ran on a short forty-metre long track around a tree in my front yard.

I thought I was very inventive in trying to stick to my goals. I was, but my fear of regaining drove my inventiveness. It was not sustainable.

When I told a friend about my fear of regaining, his response was, "Yes, you should be scared."

My friend is incredibly clever and has witnessed years of my yo-yo dieting. I assumed he was right. I have fallen off the wagon so many times. I should always watch my step and every single bump in the road before me. Discipline! That is what I need. I will diet for the rest of my life.

What does fear do? Fear makes you want to fight, or fear debilitates you and makes you freeze. Fear and constantly needing to face it makes you ultimately want to run away and give up. I decided to fight my fear — and I thought I could fight it by continuing to be perfect all the time:

I will continue to follow my eating formula to a tee.

I will exercise religiously.

I will never stray.

But I am only human. Inevitably I will fail. Somehow, I need to make peace with the reality that I cannot always be perfect. Can I just be good? Will that be enough?

The One Thing That Stands Out Most

I do not know what the beginning of my story is.

Should I start from where I first started picking up weight? Considering I was an overweight toddler and that I cannot remember any time in my life where I wasn't fat, that doesn't seem like a very logical place to start.

Do I start at the beginning of my eighty kilograms weight loss journey? That would make sense, except that my story is not about losing weight. There are more than enough diets out there. Adding to that noise would be pointless, nor is it something that I wish to do.

No, my story is about introspection. It is also about self-love, guilt, shame, fear, judgement, and so much more. My narrative is about healing. I am choosing to begin telling it from where I started to mend.

It was a Tuesday afternoon. Usually, a Tuesday afternoon is my busiest afternoon of the week. My children have swim, dance and art lessons on a Tuesday, and I have my weekly weigh-in and presentation at our group as well. But this Tuesday afternoon was not busy at all. We were still in a hard Covid lockdown and could not go anywhere outside our house. Swimming, dancing and art lessons were either all cancelled or happening online. Even my weigh-ins were virtual.

This Tuesday afternoon was relatively relaxed. I had just started reading a new book and planned to go for a run later that afternoon on my self-made and improvised running track around a tree in my front yard. Exercising in any public area was still illegal, hence the need to run within my property's perimeter.

Therapist wrote the new book I had started reading. It was an e-book that he made freely accessible on his website for the lockdown duration. He had made all his e-books freely available, but this was the first of his books that I was reading.

Strictly speaking, Therapist wasn't my therapist then. However, I chose to refer to him as such right from the onset; that is what he ultimately became. A few weeks before South Africa's president announced our nationwide lockdown, I enrolled my husband and myself on one of his courses. He is a sex therapist and a stand-up comedian, a fascinating combination.

The course I had enrolled us for was his couple's mentoring course explicitly aimed at enriching marriages or long-term relationships. Having been very happily married for almost sixteen years then, I registered for its fun and because marital happiness is not something to be taken for granted. Even, and especially, after sixteen years and four children.

So here I was reading the first bit of Therapist's book. I love reading. I also love watching videos and listening to motivational talks. I am a good reader and a good listener. I will read and listen attentively and then brew on my newfound knowledge for hours, sometimes days or even weeks.

One thing that I often find myself doing is picking "The one thing that stands out most" from a particular piece or conversation. This information highlight is not supposed to summarise the knowledge I had recently acquired. It is just the one line, phrase, word, or even concept that struck a chord with me and was now brewing in my mind.

Part of the particular piece I was reading was the story of how Therapist met his wife. This story was a beautiful, pure and virtuous tale that stood out to me. I also had my own beautiful story to tell, a bit sad and perhaps not that virtuous, but still a beautiful story.

I met my husband when I was just sixteen years old. It was the middle of my Grade Ten year and the start of a new school term. My husband and his family were new to our town and school. On that day, during assembly, our school principal asked all the new pupils, one of them being my future husband, to stand up. When I first laid eyes on him, I immediately knew that this was the man that I would marry one day; it took me a few years to convince him to share this vision with me.

During that stage of my life, I was significantly overweight and unhappy. I was also in conflict with God about my physical appearance and my lack of friends. Although I was still praying and reading my Bible at the time, I did not experience God as good. Maybe He was good to other people, but just not to me?

I was unhappy at school. I was even more miserable at home. I was confused by my teenage hormones and frustrated at what life seemed to have in store for me. Suddenly, into my life, almost out of the blue, walked this young man, who instantaneously gave my life a whole new purpose and goal. I was head over heels in love, and it was a wonderful and strange new feeling.

One of the things I did to win over my husband's heart was to diet — my very first time dieting. I thought this diet up all by myself, and it involved only eating half or less of the food that my mum prepared for me. It was a starvation diet for all intents and purposes, but it was the only plan I could think up that would not cause any additional effort on mum's part. The last thing I wanted was to do something that would not meet my mother's approval. My mum was only on my case about my weight anyhow, she welcomed me making an effort to try and lose some weight.

My dieting plan worked very well, and I lost rather nicely during the last part of my Grade Ten and for most of my Grade Eleven year. At the end of Grade Eleven, my husband and I were elected to be prefects. However, I was not selected because I was well-liked. The other students picked me to be a prefect because I did very well academically, ending at the top of my class almost every school year. During our prefect induction dinner, things between my husband and myself started taking off; we started going out "officially" at the start of Grade Twelve — I finally had a boyfriend!

During school hours, we were an item, but back at home, I would hotly deny it if my mum or dad ever raised the subject. I always worked for and desired my parents', especially my mum's approval, but my relationship with my boyfriend was not something I was willing to give up for their sake. My mum didn't want me to be involved in romantic relationships; she wanted me to focus exclusively on my studies. I felt that I was already doing exceptionally well at school and could afford another "distraction" in my life. Thus, to avoid conflict, I kept my relationship with my boyfriend a secret at home.

I went to university the year after I completed school. My boyfriend enrolled for a diploma course and lived about two blocks away from the university residence where I was staying. My university years were the best time of my life. It was the most liberating feeling to finally be in a relationship with my boyfriend without having to deny it constantly.

The youth minister at the church I was supposed to join on campus also happened to be a minister that I knew from when I was young. It was comforting to see a familiar face, and he was a wonderful person, but he also worked with my mum over the time that he still ministered at our church from when I was still in primary school. Every time we would talk, the conversation inevitably went in the direction of my mum. Our youth minister would inquire how my mum was doing and then often respond with a historical account of my mother's wonderful personality and how lucky I was to have such a mother. I couldn't keep up the facade. So I decided, in my infinite nineteen-year-old wisdom, that the best way to avoid conversations of that nature was to not go to church.

Unfortunately, and I draw this comparison with all due respect, not going to church is almost like not going to the group meetings facilitated by your weight-loss club. After a while, it becomes easy not to go. It becomes even easier not to go if you spend most of your weekends staying at your university residence because you do not want to go home where attending a church service is compulsory. When no one is there to see you not going, no one will know that you've stopped going to church. Both faith and weight loss are challenging to do entirely on your own. You need guidance from someone with more knowledge and experience, and you need the community to draw from and give back to.

The result of not going to church was that during my university years, and for years after that, I felt very far removed from God. I was a Christian, had been brought up in a Christian home. I knew my Bible reasonably well. But this was a time in my life that I felt I had no relationship with God and that "Christian" was just something I filled in when asked what my religion was.

My relationship with my boyfriend was, however, going very well. I picked up all the weight that I had lost before we started going out with interest, but it didn't seem to matter to my boyfriend at all. He loved and accepted me for who I was, not for what I looked like, and it was the most gratifying feeling in the entire world.

During my second year at university, we decided that we did not want to wait till marriage before taking our relationship to a sexual level. Did I hear you gasp at this confession of mine?

That is what I imagine people doing when reading this divulgence. Perhaps that says more about me than anyone else? Bear in mind that even today, after nearly seventeen years of marriage, we are still each others' first and only sexual partners — no mean feat for almost any couple out there. We were both taught to wait until marriage. But becoming sexually active felt like the right next step for our relationship at that stage in our lives.

A few of our friends probably knew what was going on, but we never discussed this with anyone else, especially not our parents. I didn't even discuss it with any of my friends or sisters.

Because Therapist's story in his book had made such an impression on me, and I had just finished reading it, I decided to share how my husband and I met, along with this never before divulged secret with him. The first time that I've ever told anyone else — a significant indicator to me of the level of confidence and approachability that I've already experienced at that early stage with Therapist.

Perhaps therapists are naturally inclined and trained to draw information out? Maybe my heart just felt heavy having carried such a secret for such a long time? Possibly I just wanted someone knowledgeable on the subject to confirm that I was a rotten apple? That is how I felt then. I don't know why I decided to tell him, but he replied with a message that would change my life a short while later. He said, "Great story, but please stop feeling guilty now about premarital sex."

With Therapist having started his career as a youth pastor, I expected some form of reprimand or judgement from him. The secret I shared with him was probably the biggest secret I had ever shared with anyone. The coffee stain to an otherwise near perfect marriage. Already taken aback by his reply, I said, "That is going to be a challenging thing to do."

"Why?" Therapist asked.

Did I need to explain to him that premarital sex was a sin? Certainly not. After all, he had studied theology. A big reason why I enrolled us for his course in the first place was that his practices were rooted in Christian principles — something essential to me after finally feeling that I was back to a point in my life where I have a relationship with God again.

I answered, "Because it is wrong. We were taught that sex belongs in a long-term committed relationship, such as a marriage, not in a 'just longer than two years'-relationship with your first boyfriend."

"When I listen to your and your husband's story, I hear nothing other than a long-term committed relationship. I'd like you to thank your husband for having premarital sex with you and for being faithful to you and to stop carrying this guilt," Therapist replied.

It would have been so much easier if he just started his initial reply with a reprimand. Or he has this thing he typically does where he would, to save some time, send back a thumbs-up. I would have preferred a thumbs-up reply in this case.

Suddenly my relaxing Tuesday afternoon became very interesting. I wasn't planning on doing this much thinking and introspection. Not after confessing such a big secret, which I believed to be a sin, to someone that was still a stranger to me. Couldn't he confirm that it was a sin and let me continue living with the guilt that I had done something many years ago to stain my wonderful marriage?

Already dressed for the run I was planning on doing that afternoon, I replied: "Yes, we were as committed as two twenty-year-olds could probably be to each other. But that doesn't guarantee that we would eventually have married each other. Not that marriage comes with any guarantees either. Okay, I see your point. But I cannot imagine how I will ever get to a point where I will be thankful for this or not feel guilty about it. I will have to think why this bothers me so much that I still feel troubled about it even after many years of marriage. I feel that I still need to hide this, even with both my parents already having passed away. Couldn't you just have replied initially with one of your thumbs-up replies today? I prefer those replies; they require less thinking. I have to go for a run now. That will give me some time to think. I will get back to you."

"The best way to loosen dust," Therapist said.

I suspect he already knew then how this conversation would pan out.

What followed was one of the most challenging runs I have ever done. I broke down a few times during the run as some ancient and forgotten feelings started coming back to me. Ultimately, I quit my run prematurely as I was crying too much. My run loosened too much dust and cobwebs. I would have preferred them to have remained intact.

Eventually, I replied to Therapist: "I don't think it is the premarital sex itself that bothers me. It is the secret keeping and lying that I did to my parents. And all the reasons why I feel that I needed to. I teach my children that they should wait till marriage, or at the very least for a steady, committed relationship, before engaging in any sexual activities. I aim to be as open and as honest as possible with them about sex and, if ever asked if I had waited till marriage, I would tell them the truth. I do not want to be hypocritical. I want to have this open communication channel with them and for them to feel that they can discuss these things with me, which is something I've never had with my mum."

Then Therapist said something that made me want to curl up into a tiny ball and hide for the rest of eternity.

"Okay, so now we are on a new topic: 'Your relationship with your mother'. Tell me more ..."

Playing The 'Husband Card'

I never intended to go for therapy. I never looked up numbers or email addresses for any therapists. I never asked for recommendations. It was probably the last thing I would have considered doing, if ever.

By going for therapy and committing myself to the process of it, I figured out who I truly am. Counselling gave my life back to me — something I've never experienced before. But allowing a therapist to work with me was also one of the most challenging things I have ever done. I had to give a stranger a view into the shame and hurt that formed part of my soul, and then, by default and because I am just human, I feared his judgement. Keep in mind that it is not as if we have a little door to open into our psyche. We are often not even aware of our problems ourselves; to make a stranger aware of them while at the same time facing these problems, perhaps for what might be the very first time, is hard work. You have to dig, scratch, cut, blunder out and be so vulnerable that sometimes the hurt of sharing feels more than the pain that was already there.

I still remember our second session; I was shaking so much that I could barely string a proper sentence together. I would always plan a little bit before each session, and for this session, I knew I had a colossal confession that I needed to make. I convinced myself that if I were to tell Therapist this huge secret, he was going to say, "Right, that's it! Time to refer you to another therapist."

Yet, noticing how shaken I was, he decided to start our session with a prayer and a calm word or two. His attempts at lifting the mood did help a little bit, but it didn't stop me from needing to take a few intense breaths before spilling the beans as to what was bothering me so much — which only happened towards the end of my session. Pure torture!

When Therapist asked me to tell him more about my relationship with my mother, I replied that I could not do that. There was just too much to say. I told him that I would email him with the story. I typed out the promised email that very Tuesday evening still. I couldn't sleep, and I needed to get the weight of the promised email off my chest.

Re-reading that email now, I can see for myself how much I have grown. That email was very factual and cold. I now realise how I tried to hide among the written text. At that stage, I still tried not to let Therapist see the real me. However, despite my best efforts to tell the story as factual and as emotionless as I could, he managed to see right through it and by the Friday, when he had time to read it himself, he suggested that I come to see him for a few sessions. I very strongly insisted that I did not think that was a good idea at all.

I might have been a first-time therapy patient, but I am pretty sure that therapy is not supposed to work this way around. I believe the client is supposed to contact the therapist and not the other way around. Yet, that is how it happened in my case. If it weren't for Therapist approaching me, I don't think I would've ever ended up in a place where I could get the help I needed. I would never have known that therapy was the route I was supposed to follow. I firmly believe that my and Therapist's paths were meant to intersect how and when they did. When I recollect how this all worked out, I still get goosebumps and feel a tremendous sense of gratitude.

My first objection to sessions was that the topics Therapist suggested we talked about were old wounds — ancient. I saw no advantage in raking up the past when my parents and my younger sister had already passed away. I was, however, curious as to why I never mourned my mother and sister's deaths. I believed that I was always responsible for all the work needed and thus too busy to mourn during these trying times. Therapist felt that opening up these old wounds would bring freedom and a lightness to my soul and that not wanting to talk about my past should be even more of an indication to me that I actually should. But I did not find his arguments convincing enough.

It wasn't until he played what I call the 'husband card' that I agreed. Therapist said, "Ask your husband how often he perceives you as walking with unnecessary shame and guilt. How often are you easily triggered to be on the defence immediately and overreact?"

I only admitted many months later that if it wasn't for me believing that my going for therapy was for my husband's benefit, I don't think I would've started with it in the first place. I did not consider myself worthy of going for therapy; I did believe that my husband was worthy of having an emotionally stable wife. My husband described me deciding to go for counseling rather well. He said that it was like a piece of shame bait that I fell for hook, line, and sinker.

However, therapy never was a blame game. And it is not my intention to turn my writings into a blame festival either. Dr Brené Brown said in her TED talk on the subject of shame, '(Blame is) a way to discharge pain and discomfort.' Discharge means getting rid of something. If blame is a way of getting rid of pain and discomfort, it is no wonder that so many of us do it. Unfortunately, it does not work.

My children are experts at the 'blame game'. "It wasn't me! It was …!" they scream at almost every confrontation I have when trying to find a guilty party. But ultimately, the deed had been done. Even admission of guilt is not going to change the past. The best we can do is understand the extent of the damage and repair that which is mendable.

It would be convenient to find a guilty party in my story and have them come and mend the damage done. It would be so easy to blame someone and, in one sweep of a 'Blame magic wand', discharge my pain and discomfort. But it is not as simple as that. The damage had been inflicted over many years. It could not simply be undone.

Perhaps I should have stated right from the start that one doesn't just simply pick up eighty kilograms. There has to be something seriously wrong in your life to do that to yourself. Many people tried to point that out to me over many years, but I was in denial. Others thought the problem was my lack of self-control or that I was just lazy. I chose to believe them and label myself as lazy, unmotivated or a failure. For most of my life, I thought that being fat was my genetically destined path — my lot in the genetic lottery. Diets would either work or wouldn't work; regardless, I never managed to keep any weight lost off. I always 'yo-yo'-ed back.

Only now, when I found myself at the end of a very challenging journey to lose eighty kilos, that I started searching for answers to the question of why am I always struggling with my weight. Why could I not figure this 'being slim' thing out? I have no desire to pick up all eighty kilograms again — I mean, let's not kid ourselves, losing eighty kilograms was arduous work. But I fear I am a serial yo-yo dieter. Picking that weight up again feels like it is my destiny.

I can blame no one for my weight gain — I take that all on me. No one forced me to overeat. No one chained me to a couch to prevent me from exercising. Certain circumstances placed me in a position where I felt that eating was the only thing that made sense. My pain and emotional instability also didn't just manifest themselves in the form of fat. I also have problems screaming at my children, driving, being in control, being a perfectionist, and more. However, none of my issues was so outwardly visible as being overweight. I could hide my other issues or find ways to work around them, but I could not conceal an additional eighty kilograms on my body.

There was also not just one circumstance, event, or happening that was the root of my problems. I am not even sure I have found all the sources yet. But those origins that I am aware of I am planning to discuss. Whichever roots there were, and from wherever they originated, they all come together to this: I have never felt worthy of being loved unconditionally — not even by myself. Always the loser at the "I am enough" game. I am also not convinced that I was ever actually loved unconditionally.

I believe my husband and probably my children, on most days, do love me, but those are the only people I sense that feel, or have ever felt, that way. The one time in my life when I found somebody who did love me unconditionally, I was brainwashed to believe that it was wrong, dirty, and shameful. The problem is most certainly not that I am a cold or heartless person. I love and care so much, so swiftly, and so profoundly. I give and give; I give of myself in bucket loads. And I never expect anything in return because I do not feel that I am worthy of receiving love.

When Comedy Turned Into Tears

My husband and I have always been big fans of stand-up comedy, even before we were married. Thinking about it now, my small group of friends at varsity and I all used to love comedy shows. When we worked late at night on assignments, we'd often play some stand-up comedy in the background. The later we worked, the funnier it became ...

Stand-up comedy is also definitely why my language is sometimes more "colourful" than befits a lady, one of my not-so-great characteristics. The habit of watching stand-up comedy is something my husband and I continued into our marriage and still enjoy today. We have even been to watch a few live shows over the years. It is one of the best ways to spend a night out, I believe.

When I heard about Therapist's courses for the first time, I thought they were perfect for my husband and me. With Therapist being a stand-up comedian and a sex therapist, and his courses focusing on using humour to enrich your marriage, I could envision us enjoying and benefitting from them as they seemingly fitted our lifestyle and personalities.

Therapist's courses were much more than just light entertainment. He packed a lot of educational value into them while at the same time keeping them entertaining. I wanted to partake and learn from what he had to offer fully.

Unfortunately, the Covid lockdown meant that Therapist could not perform as a stand-up comedian for live audiences at a venue anymore. Being the creative person he is, he started writing more courses for which people could enroll. Whenever he added new classes, those already partaking in his couple's mentoring program, like my husband and me, also benefited from these new courses. At the time of my first therapy session, we were already part of the mentoring program and two other online courses.

The training programs by themselves were already quite a lot to manage — and then therapy was added into the mix as well. I felt overwhelmed, but I didn't want to push pause on any of the programs we were doing then. I knew that this was Therapist's way of sustaining his business through the lockdown, and I wanted to continue supporting him. It only hit me much later why I felt such a strong need to be supportive.

My first therapy session was tough! It was probably one of the most challenging things I have ever done. I assumed that we might start with the self-and-shame-portrait I drew beforehand, but we didn't. Maybe we would've started with my drawing if I didn't tell Therapist that one of the reasons I convinced myself to come for therapy was to understand why I never mourned my mum and my sister's deaths. We took the rest of the session from there.

Therapist asked me, "Are you someone who is normally not very emotional or who struggles to show emotion?"

"No, normally, I am very emotional. When my father passed away, I did mourn his death. I even messed up his eulogy at his funeral because I was crying so much. At my mum's funeral, I didn't want to give a eulogy, mostly because I believed I would mess that up as well, but also because I struggled to mourn her death. I was just too cold towards it," I replied.

"How do you believe you messed up your dad's eulogy?"

"I was only twenty-one when my dad passed away. Despite my age, my mum and sisters felt that I was the best person to present the eulogy. I was always supposed to be the strong and exemplary one, even then. Yet, standing up there in the front of the church, I couldn't get a single word out. I was crying too much. At one stage, even the minister came to stand next to me to help. It was a mess. I messed it up. I didn't do any justice to my dad."

Therapist said I should try to imagine my dad's reaction to me standing in front of the other mourners in church trying to present the eulogy. He asked me if I could see how he would have reacted and what this reaction would have been. And all I could see was *Pride*. Although it made me feel better about the eulogy I gave all those years ago, it didn't make me regret not doing one at my mum's funeral.

Yes, I know; I probably appear as being a heartless person. You may well end up hating me for the way I felt towards my mum. And that is okay, this is my story, and that was the way I felt. Even though I did love my mum and really did love her a great deal, I don't think I've ever liked her.

After discussing my father's eulogy, it was almost as if the focus shifted intentionally to my sister's death instead of my mum's. I felt frustrated by this. Perhaps Therapist understood that the cold feeling I had towards my mum was not something to address in a first session? Maybe he thought that I would have more luck trying to work through issues I had with my sister than those I had with my mum? I am not sure, but what followed were three months of almost solely focusing on the relationship I had with my sister. Concentrating on the relationship between myself and my sister, while I believed most of my issues originated from the relationship I had with my mum, was highly frustrating. It was as if I could not move forward. I felt as if my sister was holding me back and couldn't let me go. Afterwards, I realised, with Therapist's help, that it was I who couldn't let her go.

My Younger Sister

My sister committed suicide.

The full stop at the end of the sentence above is a mental block. Whenever I come to sit and write about my sister, the sentence above is the only one I can write down. It is as if I cannot progress past the full stop. Although my sister was more than just someone who committed suicide, to me, it is the only thing defining her life.

My sister was diagnosed with manic depression about a year or so after completing school. She was also significantly overweight — obese. At the time of her death, she was more than ninety kilograms overweight. She was just eighteen months younger than I. Interestingly enough, she and Therapist differed precisely one week in age, with Therapist being just that little bit older than her.

At one stage, my sister was my best friend. But somewhere along the way, we lost each other. The morning I was meant to go to my varsity residence for our initiation week, she begged me not to leave her. But how could I stay? Going to university was my ticket out of our childhood home. I had to leave her. Things were never really the same again after that.

My husband and I moved into our first small cluster home one year into our marriage. About eighteen months after our move, I asked my younger sister if she wanted to move in with us. I did this because I felt that it would be good for her to move away from our hometown. She grabbed the opportunity and stayed with us until shortly after our second child's birth — it was then when our small three-bedroom home became too small for the five of us. My sister had an extremely close relationship with my eldest child as she would often watch him and babysit for us. She was almost like his second mum, and my son loved her as such as well. The relationship between my sister and me never mended, even though she stayed with us all those years. I was always the one that had forsaken her when she needed me.

My sister married relatively late in life. She and her husband wanted to start a family quite soon after getting married, but things didn't work out for them that way. Eventually, it became clear that they would need some form of medical help to fall pregnant. Unfortunately, my sister's obesity status and other medical problems like her extremely high blood pressure made it very dangerous for her to undergo any medical procedures to fall pregnant without losing weight first.

She was desperate to be a mum herself; it was such a big heart's desire of hers. But she could not lose the weight, and the success I had on my weight loss journey, which had started by then already, did not help our relationship either. We became even more estranged.

There was a great deal of information that my husband and I only became privy to on the day of her suicide. Because of her previous suicide attempts, after our father passed away, we were aware of her struggle with depression. We thought she had her depression under control and received the medication needed to manage it effectively. I was aware that she wanted to lose weight, and I was aware of her desire to fall pregnant.

I did not know that one of the things that she believed prevented her from losing weight was her depression medication and that that belief stopped her from continuing her medication as prescribed. We were also not aware that during her still short marriage, she attempted suicide twice. When my brother-in-law phoned my husband that Friday afternoon with the news of her suicide, we only learned then that it was already her third suicide attempt during their marriage.

Then, we learned that she lost her job months before and kept a facade intact of her still appearing to be employed. We also discovered that she shopped compulsively, buying baby items for that 'one day' when she would have a child of her own until they were in debt. All of this new information was a great deal of information to take in on the same day you've lost your baby sister.

My brother-in-law was furious — an understatement actually — I have never before seen anyone so livid. I felt so sorry for him; my sister's death hurt him significantly. I love my brother-in-law; I've known him for many, many years. He is also a software engineer, and the three of us — me, him and my husband — had worked together for several years. I was also the one that introduced my sister to him. Her death might've left me cold towards her, but it did not make me feel cold towards my brother-in-law. I wanted to help and ease some of his pain.

I didn't expect him to expect me to help sort through all her personal belongings, as well as all the purchased baby items, though. When he asked me if I would sell the baby products to help with some of the debt he and my sister had accumulated, I was even more stunned. He needed the capital from the baby products as soon as possible; otherwise, there wouldn't be funds for my sister's funeral. How does one process something like that? Is this type of pressure even fair? I could've refused, but honestly, how could I? My sense of responsibility would've ridden me with guilt if I did.

The sequence of events around my sister's death was as follows:

My sister passed away on a Friday.

My brother-in-law had his mum and sister pack up all her earthly belongings by the Sunday afterwards and then dropped them off at our house. I am not exaggerating if I say everything — from the shampoo that she used to her makeup, her clothes, her shoes, even her menstrual products — everything. It was a mountain of stuff.

On the Wednesday after my sister's death, my brother-in-law started dropping off all the baby products at our house. The baby products filled up more than three rooms inside their house. When placed in our home, it was like a mountain of goods that I had put in our living and patio areas. It was a momentous task, placed solely on my shoulders and all this, not even a week after losing my sister. Of course, I never mourned her death. Circumstances then made it impossible for me to take the time that I needed to grieve. I was also presented with so many well-kept secrets while learning about her suicide that I became furious and filled with anger myself. Time and anger became mental blocks to my grieving.

So when Therapist started talking about my sister, one of the first things that he said I should try and do is imagine myself going up to heaven to speak with my sister. It was then that I asked him, "But what if I don't believe that she's gone to heaven?"

Therapist's response to this was: "Wow."

He then continued to explain that her going to heaven, or not, was a situation between herself and God. I had to believe the best-case scenario, the one that brought me the most peace.

After sorting out the location of this imaginary trip, he continued to explain that I needed to imagine myself talking to her and that I had to tell her all the anger I harboured towards her. Get angry, scream, shout, swear — that was his assignment to me. I couldn't do this assignment. The imagined scenario didn't feel real enough to me, and I did not know how to make it feel more believable — I sucked at therapy! Perhaps I didn't want Therapist to see all that anger I harboured in me? Because I struggled with this exercise in session, Therapist asked me to let my anger out by writing my sister a letter instead.

The letter weighed heavily on my mind for the rest of that week. Our session was on a Tuesday, and it was my thirty-ninth birthday the following Thursday. It was probably one of the worst birthdays I've ever had. Not only was I still broken from my therapy session, but I had leave scheduled for Thursday and Friday — leave that I could not make use of entirely. When booking that leave at the start of the year, the original plan was to go somewhere over that weekend. But with Covid lockdown still in place, the furthest trip we could take was to our local grocery store. I decided not to cancel the leave but to try to make the most of those two days and rest well — rest is a relative term for a mother of four under the best conditions.

During this "rest" that which I wished to say in the letter started brewing, it felt like a pressure cooker about to pop its lid. Late on that Friday evening and early on Saturday morning, I was writing. For the first time, I was doing something that somehow resembled journaling. Most of Therapist's courses had journaling assignments. I never did any of these. My default reaction to them was usually to roll my eyes and say to myself, "Yeah, right, as if that is ever going to happen." I even confessed this to Therapist later on when I fully understood the therapeutic benefits of journaling.

Below is the letter I wrote to my sister:

*   *   *

I am not even sure where or how to start this letter. "Be angry" was the assignment. Angry, what is angry? I know I was angry. Am I still angry? Probably. Otherwise, I would not be writing this at all — right? Will I be angry forever? Probably. I've never shared this anger with anyone. Not like anyone else was interested in hearing about it anyway. Nobody was interested in hearing how it is going on my side of the world. Everybody felt sorry for you. Some felt sorry for me. Everybody felt sorry for your husband — yes, especially your husband. Being sorry does not help anything or anybody. "Sorry" is an empty word that people use when they do not know what to say. Sympathy means nothing and solves nothing. It can fix no problems. It is to no one's advantage.

"Sorry for your loss" — what loss? I lost you while you were still alive. Because you were my sister, you were biologically closer to me than anybody else on earth, yet you wanted nothing to do with me. You worked me out of your life. You were a closed book. You never wanted to share anything. You were hurting, but you refused to share any of that pain with somebody who could potentially have helped you. You didn't want help. I tried so hard to reach out to you — so hard. And so often. But you took my advice and my attempts at helping and spat on them. You wanted none of it. And you made sure that I knew that you didn't want my help. You waved that fact in front of my face and taunted me with it.

You never treated me like a sister. How many people did you not turn against me? You were always the victim. People just needed to feel sorry for you. You were always the unfortunate one. The unlucky one. Do you know what? Luck doesn't have anything to do with it. I wasn't lucky when I got better marks at school than you — I worked hard for them. I still remember how much attention you paid to your schoolwork. What you sow, you will reap; a proverb you never really seemed to understand. "I am not as lucky as you!" it was one of your favourite things to say. Whenever life didn't work out for you, your lack of luck was somehow my fault as well.

I wasn't lucky to be successful at losing weight. You blocked me on social media when I started to share about my weight loss journey, and then I couldn't even see the posts you made about drugs and suicide before your suicide. You always expected me to support you and your business, but you never showed me any support in return. My goal always was to help you. I tried sensitively to pull you into my journey and help you with your weight problems, but you had only bad things to say about my choice of a weight loss program. That was an insensitive thing to do to someone trying to lose weight herself. You wanted me to fail. If it were someone else, I would've given them an earful, but because it was you — I tolerated it. Did you ever realise that it wasn't easy for me either? You were never there for me. Did you think it was easy to attempt to lose eighty kilograms? Despite all your nasty comments and purposeful sabotage, I still tried to pull you in and help you. You never did the same for me. Neither you nor your husband showed me any support.

You excluded me whenever and in whichever way you could. Even at your wedding, you made sure I understood that I was not welcome. Even though I was the reason you and your husband met. Even though he and my husband are best friends, you made sure I understood that the only reason I was there was so you could have some cute flower girls and pageboys.

Ah, the children — my children. That is probably the thing I am most angry about, that I allowed you to form such a big part of their lives. My eldest loved you so much, but so did all the others. Yet you only ever seemed to care about my eldest. His heart was broken into a million pieces when he found out that you've passed away. He had to process this news the same week he was due to write his first final exams. If you were going to pick a day to die, why do that to a child? You broke him. He loved you, but you took that love and shattered it onto the floor. Why that weekend?

The morning before my youngest's last school concert and the girls' dance concert. Why over that incredibly hectic weekend? Was it your way to show us that none of that mattered to you? I always invited you to these events, at no cost — you hardly ever came. Only if it were something for my eldest, then you would make a plan. How do you think that made the other children feel?

I am sorry that you never became a parent yourself. I struggle to understand why you deemed it necessary to buy so much baby stuff? You were an accountant; you should have known better. What were you hoping to achieve by doing that? Wait, I know — you dragged yourself and your husband into so much debt so you could list it as one of the reasons in your suicide letter, right?

The same letter that didn't even make a single mention of me. Even in one of your final acts, you forgot about my existence. You never felt it necessary to include or mention me as a part of your life. Yet, I was the one who was stuck with the job of selling all your compulsive purchases. Your husband wanted to get rid of everything "you" as soon as possible. Then somehow, I was the one who ended up with all the shit. Suddenly I was good enough. In one way or another, I am usually the one who is stuck with all the shit. I don't even enjoy shopping. I hate hoarding, debt and senseless buying. I was that one stuck with mountains and mountains and mountains of shit, with your husband looking in my direction for a solution. Do you know that he told my husband — which seems to be how I discover most things — there wasn't even enough money for you for a funeral? Do you realise the pressure a statement like that placed on my shoulders?

Do you know how much the selling of your senseless, compulsive purchases took out of me? How many evenings, weeks — and that for a sister to whom I was nothing. You weren't even dead for two days, and I already started to sort out the stuff. Mostly on my own. It took days. All the while, I was having my own house to run and a young teenager busy with exams. I had to figure out prices, advertising, delivery, everything. Selling your purchases was never something I wanted to do. It was your choice to take your life — not mine. I never wanted you dead. It was your choice to buy all the baby items — not mine. You also purchased so senselessly. It just goes to show that you never listened to any advice I ever offered you.

Anyway, who buys baby items before even being pregnant? Why did you hide these purchases from everyone? Why did no one tell us of your previous suicide attempts? A big part of me wants to ask you, "Are you happy now that you've been successful at taking your own life? Is this what you wanted?"

Why did you say nothing when you lost your job? Why all the secrets? Why didn't you ask anyone for help? Why did you cut me out of your life? Why didn't you ever listen to any of my advice? Why were you so stubborn? Why were you so cold towards me? I never felt supported. Why didn't you ever show interest in my life?

Things could have been so much better if you were not so proud and stubborn. You had everything, but you were too blind to see it. You had a husband who worshipped you. You were everything and more to him. Your husband loved you so much. You had a sister who loved you and so badly wanted to help. You had nieces and nephews who adored you. You had people who were willing to help and support you. But you decided that you were not enough. You decided that we were not enough for you. Nothing would ever have been enough for you. You died the same way that you lived, selfishly. And in the process, you broke the rest of us.

Mourning

It took about two months before Therapist and I discussed the letter I wrote to my younger sister. His main comment was that he could see I felt excluded from her life. He believed that getting the anger out was an important step.

I asked, "Do you think I will ever get to a point where I will mourn her death?"

"Yes, one day you will."

"But I am not strong enough to do that. My dad's passing already broke me. I cannot go through something like that again."

"Mourning your sister's death will probably not be like that. You might watch a movie or hear a new song that will make you cry. Only afterwards you will realise that those tears were for your sister."

On the Saturday after the session we discussed my letter, we had a booking to watch an online comedy show by one of our favourite South-African comedians. My husband and I also purchased a ticket for Therapist for this show. Therapist was not keen on hosting an online event, and I was hoping that experiencing a presentation from another comedian might change his mind.

By the Monday after the show, I had still not heard any feedback from him about the online event and what he thought of it. I found this strange, so I messaged him. He replied that the show was good, but the online format would not work. I was expecting a response along the lines of "The online show was awesome (which I thought it was). I think it is something worth investigating." When that wasn't the case, I was disappointed. I hoped experiencing the online format for himself might be the solution to him continuing with his stand-up comedy. I just wanted to help.

I shared that feeling of disappointment with him. His reaction to my disappointment greatly surprised me. He said that I do not need to help him, nor should I feel like I need to. He added that he observed some strange form of power-dynamic between the two of us, almost like transference. Because he helps me, I feel that I need to help him. Instead, I should rather lean into and embrace the discomfort that comes from our therapy sessions and not feel like I need to do something in return.

I had no idea what transference was, so I went to look it up. Transference is when a therapy client directs emotions meant for someone else towards their therapist. After reading up on transference a lot that Monday evening, I realised something substantial: what Therapist had described wasn't "almost" like transference. It was precisely transference. I also knew who the "someone else" was meant to be the recipient of my feelings. There was only one other person in my life that I always felt I needed to help. I was directing emotions I had for my sister towards Therapist.

Suddenly a lot of things started making sense! I mailed Therapist with this realisation. He responded that I should realise that this was a breakthrough for me. I felt responsible for my sister's death. In my mind, I was saying, "No, I am not. She refused my help." But my emotions were saying something completely different. My feelings were saying that I should have done more and tried harder. I needed to free myself from the responsibility I felt towards my sister's death. There was nothing I could have or should have done to prevent her death.

On the first read of Therapist's response, his words didn't register with me. But the more I allowed them to brew and settle into my soul, the more the realisation anchored in my heart and mind. And the freer I started feeling from the massive responsibility I'd taken on my shoulders for most of my life. That afternoon I went for my usual afternoon run — the best way to loosen dust — when it suddenly hit me, out of the blue — I longed for my little sister. And I don't just yearn for her a little. I miss her a whole lot! But I crave the person that could still get excited with me about things like birthday parties. The version that thought I was the funniest and always laughed at my silly jokes. I needed the sister that was always so willing to help me. The close relative who would completely understand when I talked about things from our childhood. I wanted the baby sister that I didn't have to worry over so much. And with this realisation, I couldn't run anymore, so I ended up slowly walking my usual route in tears.

Mourning my sister's death was not like Therapist said it would be at all. It was painful. The thing with mourning someone almost two years later is that other people don't understand. It is not the natural order or way of doing things. Perhaps I am not an average person? However, the important thing was that I managed to mourn my sister's death. Even though my eyes were still burning by the following Friday afternoon, I felt so much better and "lighter".

Because Therapist also freed me from any obligation I felt towards him, I decided to pause all our enrolled courses. It was difficult for me to halt these courses — my husband and I enjoyed them. I registered us for them in the first place to do something together that was mutually beneficial and for the enrichment of our marriage. I always said the mentoring courses were for both of us, but therapy was for me. Pausing these courses felt like a selfish thing to do, but I needed to do that to get focus on my therapy sessions.

When Therapist asked me: "Are you someone who is normally not very emotional, or who struggles to show emotion?" I don't think he realised just how much of an emotional person I was. I feel so quickly and easily. I wear my heart on my sleeve.

Therapist was so similar to my sister — in many ways. It was as if she had come back from death to haunt me.

When he talked about his struggles with depression, I thought *No ...*

When he answered my messages with his thumbs-up replies, I thought *This cannot be ...*

I believe in miracles. I see miracles happening through people, such as Therapist, destined to cross one's path and used as instruments. Devices for good; tools for healing — but also to hurt?

He gave me a taste of the way a sibling relationship perhaps could have been. He was someone to share with, who'd listened, understand

and could relate. I longed for that type of relationship in my life. I found myself feeling comfortable, safe and opening up. Perhaps for the first time, I shared and became aware of my desire to share. I realised how much I needed help. I also realised that I have a tremendous amount of love to give.

I have friends; I am not the loner I was in school anymore. But maybe I use the term *friend* too casually? I have people that I will invite over for a visit, or perhaps share something with or even ask for help at times if I can see no other way. They are friends, but they aren't "sibling-type" of friends. It took someone, like Therapist, to come along and treat me the way that he treated me to make me realise what was missing in my life. It was through him that I realised how much I missed my sister.

Maybe if my sister wasn't so sick? Perhaps if she didn't take her own life? Maybe that was what our relationship could've been? My failed relationships with both my mother and my sister caused massive empty spaces in my life. I was never aware of these empty voids before, and suddenly I could see them everywhere. Unknowingly Therapist filled at least one of them. Or did I suck him into it? I transferred the feelings I had towards my sister onto him. It was such an easy thing to do. Was it a trap? If it was, I fell right into it. I thought I was smarter than that. I felt stupid, tricked and taken for a fool. Or was this the way it was always supposed to play out? A divine plan?

When we labelled this problem as 'transference', it became a wall. I felt as if I was doing something wrong. As if I was a bad person for feeling the way I felt.

Transference was a horrible word — a big no-no. Something that could not, should not and were not allowed to happen. Transference meant Therapist needed to terminate my therapy sessions — that is what he was trained to do in this situation. Luckily for me, he didn't end our sessions right away, and I am incredibly thankful for that, as we hadn't even started looking into my relationship with my mum at that stage. Ultimately, however, it did cause our therapy journey to come to an end.

If I have to be completely honest, I believe that Therapist used transference as an excuse to end our sessions for him not to hurt me even more at that stage. Therapy curriculums might teach therapists to terminate sessions once transference occurs – I had no therapy experience, so I was none the wiser. But the truth was that I was forming an unhealthy attachment to him. If we were to ignore it, our relationship would have become toxic and harmful.

I asked my husband one evening what it was that he would miss when either of his parents or his brother were to pass away. What was the loss that he would mourn? His answer boiled down to love; it was the love he would miss. A person who he loved and who loved him in return would be gone.

Besides my husband and my children, I do not feel that I have or have had any other unconditional love relationships in my life. I believe that there should have been, but there were none. Besides my husband, there was never someone else to share with or who would get excited about anything with me. There was no one who I knew cared deeply for me and would always have my back. The person I would want to share a new blog post with, whom I know would read it. Or someone I would message first with some good news. I have never had that; it has always just been my husband and me against the world. My husband will talk to his parents or his brother almost weekly, and before Covid, we used to see them monthly. I, however, never phone or visit with anyone, nor does anyone call me either. I have no one.

The rejection of my emotional transference made me relive some of the rejection I had experienced from my mum and my sister. It was beyond painful to go through that again. This time it bored holes into the very essence of me. This time I knew what it was that I was missing.

In retrospect, coming to the end of my therapy sessions was the best thing that could have happened. Back then, it did not feel like it, but now I realise that it forced me to start doing therapy by myself. Most of this book was born out of that "own therapy".

I am not willing to go for therapy ever again for the sole reason that I believe if I let someone get so close to my emotional hurt again, I will inevitably form an unhealthy attachment. I am not willing to risk that – I have decided it is better and safer to make peace with never having such a person in my life. My husband will have to continue to be my everything, and he does a stellar job.

That is also why I write and why I run. Both paper and the tarmac are patient, non-judgemental, cannot respond, nor reject. The road doesn't care if I run on it twice a day or once every two weeks. Paper doesn't care how much I write or how much I've erased. I can cry while writing or running and feel that I have had some form of outlet. I can express all the emotions that I wish to get out, sending them off into a safe mental space. It is a space where I can give some of my love but not risk being hurt or rejected. A wonderful byproduct of my running is my fitness and muscle tone, and the byproduct of my writing is a written piece of work that can serve as an inspiration to others.

Emotional Eating

For the most significant part of my life, I thought my weight problem was purely a lack of food knowledge or a lack of well-formed healthy eating habits. Both my parents were obese. Being overweight was what was modelled to me while growing up. I was never encouraged to partake in any sport or exercise. The food we ate was a diet of rice, potatoes, stewed meat, and baked or cold puddings from a bazaar. Vegetables always had butter and sugar added and tasted like dessert. The food knowledge I acquired while growing up was the food knowledge I took into adulthood and how I continued to cook for years. Quite clearly, the food we ate during my childhood was wrong, and it was easy for me to blame my upbringing for my weight problems.

As my first diet, I just ate half or less of all my meals. My first diet worked but was not sustainable. Over many years, I have tried almost every known diet to solve my weight problem. Some of the diets I was successful at losing weight on, some diets gave me no results, and others were utterly impossible to follow or unsustainable. Ultimately, every single diet that I've tried, without exception, caused me to end up at a point where I weighed more than when I had started the eating plan. I am not stupid; I did learn from all my mistakes. Every diet taught me a tad more about how I was supposed to eat, which foods worked for weight loss, which foods to avoid, how to balance meals, and so on. Over time, I had a reasonably good idea of what was required to lose weight; I was rather good at losing weight. But good food knowledge didn't solve my weight problem.

I don't believe I am the only obese person ever to have thought that my weight problem was because I did not know how to eat. I am convinced that most overweight people believe that the solution to their problem is in their next diet. I thought that myself, diet after diet, after diet. When you want to lose weight, you start a diet. It is as "simple" as that.

I think the world is incredibly cruel to people struggling with their weight. It has become more evident to me now after losing weight myself. Advertisements across every imaginable platform bombard us with dieting information. It is a constant reminder that people out there are successful at managing their weight, but we are not. It is as if there are people "out there" who know what the secret is to losing weight and staying thin, but it has turned into this massive money-making scheme that lures you in and then spits you out, weighing more than what you started.

I could maybe explain my weight problem away by believing that I was simply genetically predisposed to being overweight. Oh, how I wish for that to be true. Being one-hundred-and-seventy-four centimetres tall and wearing a UK size nine shoe, I will never be petite. It would have been so easy to embrace my hugeness if it resulted from my genetic makeup. I could use that as an excuse never to attempt a diet in the first place. But my health was suffering because of my excess weight and not because of my natural build. While being big was in my genes, being fat was not.

Finally, after years of fighting the weight loss battle, I lost weight and reached my goal weight — something that had never happened to me before. I feared regaining those eighty kilograms. My way of controlling that fear was to weigh myself every day and stick to my diet as religiously as possible. I realised that it was only a matter of time before I would snap. A successful maintenance and eating plan needs some breathing space — mine had none. I refused to allow myself to live.

I wanted to discuss my fear of regaining weight with Therapist. The first time we talked about it, he said that the solution to freeing myself from this fear was so simple. I merely had to understand what it was that caused me to pick up weight in the first place. If I could understand that, I would realise that I am not the same person who picked up those eighty kilograms. If I could do that, I would lose the fear of regaining.

"But I've always been overweight!" I exclaimed, "And when I did manage to lose a bit, I always regained it — with interest."

"Well, in that case, you will have to figure out what the emotions are that cause you to eat compulsively," he said.

"My what? My emotions? No, it is not my emotions that cause me to eat. I am not an emotional eater." I said.

He insisted, saying, "You cannot, as a rational human being, claiming to be within full emotional control, decide to start eating compulsively, thus sabotaging yourself and your weight loss or maintenance efforts. The problem has to be with your emotions. Let's try to list the emotions that get you to the point where you feel that you might as well give up and eat."

When Therapist first started talking about emotional eating, I felt lost, in denial. It was almost as if a new game had come into play, and I didn't know the rules or how to play it. I knew the weight loss game. Over the years, I had become quite an expert. The emotional eating game was unknown to me, and I did not see myself as an emotional eater. In my mind, I saw 'Emotional Eating' as this person crying in a corner on a bed or couch wolfing down ice cream and chocolate bars. My imagined picture of what an emotional eater looked like was not something I could identify with — never has it been me. I believed in control. I always have everything, including my emotions, under control.

I wanted to give this therapy journey my best shot and perhaps, in a way, prove Therapist wrong. I see my entire therapy journey as mentally drawing up this list in retrospect. Not that we ever ended up with a final, comprehensive list. No, a list was never the goal. The goal was to become more reflective and self-aware to identify my emotional problems' roots and heal them. In the beginning, I interpreted the drawing up of this list very literally. I put down things like helplessness, feeling overwhelmed, or sad, but nothing I listed felt convincing to me. I was sure that my strong willpower and mindset was enough to overcome all the emotions I faced until one particular Thursday ...

Over the lockdown, my husband's employer started doing online cook-a-long sessions to boost company morale — our first time joining would have been that specific Thursday. Our cook-a-long menu was a Beef Wellington, fondant potatoes, a parsnip purée, and a red wine jus, and our session was going to be hosted by Roxy Wardman, South Africa's reigning MasterChef winner at that time. I looked forward to it so much.

We had purchased all our ingredients for this cook-a-long. Because cooking during the week is my responsibility, I prepared everything for that evening's meal before starting my workday, as I always did. As I sat at my desk in the home office to start work, loadshedding notifications started pouring in. Loadshedding is a scheduled power interruption to reduce the load on our electricity generating plants. South Africans can sometimes go for months without any loadshedding and suddenly have loadshedding again without prior warning.

Murphy's law would have it that our power was due to be off that evening. I started panicking. We were not going to be able to join the cook-a-long without electricity. What else was I supposed to make for supper? I did not have a plan B; I only had plan A. And if I were to keep the already bought ingredients for the next day, what would I make with them? I had no idea how to make any of the dishes planned for the cook-a-long. I looked at the ESP app, the most popular loadshedding schedule cellphone application we have available to us, the part that says "Check your schedule, plan your day", and I thought of a few appropriate cuss words. I mean — seriously — I already had my day planned.

I was sitting at my desk, cell phone in my hand, mortified and worried. My husband's desk is next to mine, and he bore the brunt of my frustration but had no solutions to offer. In the uncertainty of that moment, I got up from my desk. As if driven by some external force, I walked to my kitchen with the sole purpose of looking for something to eat. I had just eaten breakfast. I was not hungry. There was no logical reason for me to want to eat something at that moment. Standing by my kitchen island, it suddenly dawned on me. Therapist was right! I am an emotional eater.

For the first time, I realised how people numb using food. How easy, mindless and ludicrous, and yet perfectly sensible it was. Ever since that realisation, things have fallen more and more into place for me.

I realised I had some severe emotional issues. Such severe emotional problems that I would pick up eighty kilograms again, with interest, if I couldn't figure out how to solve those issues.

On that Thursday, I was feeling out of control of my situation. I didn't know which way to turn or what plan to make. I could not see a way out, and it made me reach for something over which I had control. Maybe I couldn't see a way out for supper that evening, but I could eat something right then and there. Perhaps a way to escape to a happy place for long enough to figure out a plan? I understood I try to numb what I am feeling with food, and, for the first time, I saw how I did it. For the first time, I had a clear, mindful view of a mindless action.

I could no longer blame my weight problems on a lack of knowledge. Weigh-Less, along with years of dieting experience, had given me all the information I would ever need on healthy, balanced eating. I couldn't blame my problems on bad habits any longer. I had more than three years of weight loss and weight maintenance to form good, healthy habits. I could not blame my genes. I did not inherit my fat.

I also realised why I do so well on a diet. A diet tells me precisely what to do. And I love that; I love being in control. Rules, steps and structure, and instructions are control. I like a plan, have always loved a plan. My problems arise at the moment when I am not in control. The sole reason I had been able to maintain my loss up to that point was that I still followed my eating formula. I still weighed regularly — daily if I felt I needed to. I still controlled my weight with my strong willpower. I was still on a diet.

It is fascinating that somewhere right at the start of my therapy journey, Therapist made this statement to me; he said, "It must be so tiring to always be so perfect at everything. I want to know how you handle failure or what happens when you do fail."

I replied, "I don't start anything if I know I will fail. When I do start something, then I will be successful. And I won't stop until I am."

I was still a stranger to him then. He knew nothing about me, and yet he also knew everything. I must have worn a big sign on my forehead or something.

To illustrate the problems that I have with surrendering control of a situation to me, Therapist once assigned an exercise directly to my husband — just so the message would not get lost in translation. The assignment was that, for a few hours, my husband had to do absolutely everything for me. During this time, I had to keep quiet, not complain, and let him do what he felt the right thing was to do using his discretion.

One Sunday morning, before our church service, my husband washed me, dressed me, fed me — he did everything for me.

I was surprised by how much this exercise bothered me. Just the thought of what was to come kept me awake from early that morning, thinking, "Perhaps I should wash my hair?" or "Maybe I should brush my teeth?"

I was also surprised by the gentleness with which my husband handled the situation. I expected him not to take the assignment seriously or joke about it. My expectation of how my husband was going to act illustrates how I always anticipate the worst reaction from other people, even from the person I trust most in this world.

Unfortunately, the solution to emotional problems is not to make sure that you never feel that emotion again. There was no way for me to ensure that I am always in charge of every situation. Being constantly in control is a highly tiring way to live — impossible even. I had to figure out the roots of my emotional problems — and they had become deeply rooted in my soul over many years. We had to scratch them open and try to heal them, one by one. Therapist kept referring to these as being my emotional black holes. I needed to find them and heal them by filling them up with something other than food. Trauma cannot heal without being acknowledged first.

Repeatedly numbing our emotions with something external, letting ourselves surrender control to the substance we are using to drug them with and then doing all this mindlessly and ultimately at the expense of ourselves — this is an addiction. An addiction always comes at a significant cost; It can steal from your health, family, joy, and marriage — every single thing you hold near and dear.

The usual way to address addiction is by withdrawing from the substance — like alcohol, drugs or cigarettes. I am addicted to food. I will always be addicted to food. But I cannot withdraw food from my life. Some people try to subclass a food addiction further by calling it a sugar, fat, or carb addiction. Subclassing does not work — in the same way, sub-classing alcoholics into wine, whiskey and brandy addicts does not make any sense. If I cannot manage my addiction by withdrawing from food or certain food groups, then the best thing I can do for myself is manage that which causes me to go into my mindless eating mode. I revert to an irrational eating mode because of my emotions. I am an emotional eater — the best I can ever hope to be is a recovering emotional eater.

Born Wrong

My relationship with my mother started the day that I was born. Maybe that sounds like an obvious statement? Doesn't everyone's relationship with their mother begin when they are born? Probably, but I got the feeling of being "wrong" right from the day of my birth.

When I was born, my mother needed an emergency C-section. Those days, the lay of the medical land was to perform a longitudinal cut across the abdomen. Unfortunately for my mum, her wound became infected and septic. After months of struggling for her incision to heal, my mum was left with debilitating abdominal hernias when it eventually did.

My mother never directly blamed me for her hernias, but whenever she would tell the story of how her hernias came to be, it would always go something like this, "On the day that Mart-Mari was born — " It didn't take rocket science for me to figure out that I was to blame.

Perhaps this whole situation would have been okay if my mother's hernias only caused her a slight inconvenience. Unfortunately, it wasn't like that. My mum suffered immensely from them. She would sometimes be in bed for days trying to push back intestines trapped by hernias. The risk was that she would not be successful at pushing them back and that the trapped intestine would cause a blockage.

It was a life-threatening situation. I have so many memories of hours spent praying in our house for my mum to become better when she was having one of her hernia episodes, all the time believing that I was to blame.

The irony of the situation was that when I was more or less thirty years old, I too was diagnosed with an abdominal hernia. Initially, my doctor could only identify one hernia, but later on, more developed. My mum was still alive then, but I never told her about my hernia diagnosis. Firstly, my relationship with my mother wasn't great, and secondly, I convinced myself that she would somehow find a way to blame my eldest daughter, my second born, for my hernias. I did not want my daughter to grow up with the same narrative that I did.

For my eldest daughter's birth, we were hoping for a VBAC. I am extremely anti-C-section, for obvious reasons, but I had already required an emergency C-section for my eldest child's birth. Advances in medical technology had made it possible for me to try again for a vaginal delivery after a transverse C-section incision.

This time around, I was set on doing things better and was determined to have a vaginal birth. I found a natural birth clinic and a midwife practice. I lost a lot of weight, about thirty-five kilograms, before and during my pregnancy with my eldest daughter. I went into labour with her at forty weeks and six days. My water broke early, but labour progressed very slowly. About twenty hours after my water broke, we noticed that my daughter had her first stool in utero, and she started going into distress. The only option then was another emergency C-section.

Because the decision to operate was so rushed, the epidural anaesthesia failed, and they had to place me under general anaesthesia. For my daughter's birth, she had to be pushed back up the birth canal a little way before they could remove her via the bikini cut. All in all, it was a very traumatic and rushed experience. Of all the C-sections I had, this recovery took me the longest time.

I also developed post-natal depression after my daughter's birth, which eventually passed. The depression, unfortunately, caused me to not go back to my Weigh-Less group meetings, and I 'yo-yo'-ed again, regaining all the weight I had lost before her birth.

The period after my daughter's birth was not the best time of my life, yet when I was diagnosed with a para-umbilical hernia, my first instinct was still to protect my daughter. I wasn't sure if her birth did somehow cause my hernia, but I wasn't for one second going to let her grow up believing that it did, nor was I going to allow my mother the opportunity to or tell her a story like that. My hernia diagnosis was just another piece of information I would keep a secret. Keeping this secret from my mum also meant keeping it a secret from everyone that knew my mother. I was good at keeping secrets; that is what I have done my entire life.

After my hernia diagnosis, I still had two more pregnancies. And I just kept gaining weight. My mum passed away before my fourth pregnancy, never knowing that I had also struggled with hernias.

I started the weight loss journey that I lost eighty kilograms a few years after my youngest was born. I started this weight loss journey solely because I needed an operation to repair my hernias. My doctor wasn't even willing to refer me to a surgeon if I didn't lose weight. I firmly believe that my determination to lose weight was fuelled to a great degree by my desire not to let my children grow up with memories of me being sick. I did not want to become my mum!

By the end of the first year on my weight loss program, I had already lost enough weight for my doctor to consider me a candidate for the operation, and she referred me to a surgeon. The surgeon wanted me to lose a little more, but about four months after being referred, I finally had the operation. I was ecstatic and determined to lose the remainder of my excess weight to get to my goal weight. I'd already experienced the benefits of weighing less and wanted more of those advantages. I desired to find out what it felt like to reach my goal weight.

During the final post-operative appointment with my surgeon, I asked him if he perhaps knew what could have caused my hernias and how I could prevent them from reoccurring.

I will never forget his words: "Given the nature and the way your hernias presented and taking into consideration that your mother also struggled with hernias, it is most likely genetic. A weak gastric membrane probably runs in your family."

My initial therapy assignment, my self-and-shame-portrait, turned out to be very important as we kept referring back to it in our sessions. The idea was to scratch out images as I became aware of them not being my guilt or shame to carry. One of the images I drew was of my mum being sick in her bed, and another was of my dad's hands in prayer. At one stage, my husband, who often sat with me discussing these sketches, felt very strongly that I needed to cross these specific images out. He reasoned that I knew now that my mum's sickness wasn't my fault and I should cross them out as they were not my shame or guilt to bear. But I never felt then that I could do that.

I tried to explain my moral dilemma like this. Imagine you were in prison for thirty-seven years believing you were guilty of a crime. One day you were released and told that actually, you were never guilty. Do you think you would be able to move on from that? Of course not. I needed to do a few things before putting this behind me.

Firstly, I needed to understand what my belief that I was responsible for my mum's hernias had stolen from me and what damage that belief had done. In my case, it stole my sense of self-worth. It made me feel that it would have been better for everyone, my mum, dad, and older sister if I had never been born. Those feelings had other ripple effects throughout my life.

Secondly, I needed to free myself from that guilt and shame and honestly believe it was never my fault.

And finally, I needed to forgive my mum for making me feel that it was my fault. More importantly, I needed to ask her for forgiveness, which is tricky to do if your mother has already passed away. Maybe she never said it was my fault, but she also never denied it. I believe that she must have felt that her struggling with hernias was my fault and that even if it wasn't, she never knew that. She was not privy to the information I received after she already died.

This particular shame was so different from all the other shame I carried with me. It is the original shame and the birthplace of every other part of my shame. It affected someone else's life immensely as it created a complex dynamic between myself and my mother, which made me feel like I had done her harm. She also believed that I did, perhaps without realising it herself. All of this affected our relationship right from the outset.

The last thing that Therapist suggested to me in a therapy session was to say that I was sorry. He said, "In your thoughts or prayers or in whatever way you feel you can communicate the message, just try to apologise to your mother for the huge amount of pain that she believed

Eighty Kilos of Shame

you caused her."

Eighty Kilograms Of Shame

There was nothing I wanted more than a good relationship with my mother. I craved it. I desired someone to confide in, who would love me unconditionally, not judge or hurt me and who would always be there for me — someone other than my husband. In spurts or over short periods, I experienced that type of relationship with my sisters. Still, it was nothing of substance and not the norm or defining characteristic of our relationship. I had a relationship like that with my father, but he lived behind my mum's mask so much that I never really felt comfortable confiding in him about anything either. I also had no other close family I could confide in from time to time.

Not only did I not have a good relationship with my mother, but I was also afraid of her. I was still scared of her even after she passed away ...

Because I could not have the relationship with my mum that I desired to have, I pretended to have it. I had a photograph of the two of us, along with a letter that she wrote to me on my wedding day, framed and hung up in my kitchen — a prominent place in my house. It was one of the first things you would see when walking into my home, and I saw it every morning as well.

I would never divulge anything about my mum or our relationship with anybody. My younger sister tried talking to an outside person about my mum many years ago. I never heard the entire story from that conversation, but I gathered the person she confided in did not take her seriously. She should not have gone to someone from our hometown.

You see, my mum had a fantastic reputation. It must have appeared as if I had the perfect mother. There was nothing she couldn't do; she excelled at everything she did. My mother was amazingly talented. She could cook, bake, sew, garden, knit, crochet, organise, keep house, and do it all to perfection. She found the time to volunteer at almost every school and church event. She was one of the most hands-on people I have ever known. My mum's personality naturally attracted others; her vast social circle was a testimony of her charming character. She made friends seemingly without any effort. Perhaps her full outside-of-the-house schedule allowed her ample time in the company of others?

My mum was also the religious head of our household. I understand society expects it to be the man of the house, but it wasn't like that in our case. My father's role was to support my mum and all her religious activities and rituals. My mum portrayed this perfect spiritual relationship. I grew up with my mum being one of our church's Sunday school teachers. I was even in her class at one stage. She was a superb teacher, and all the Sunday school children loved her, but she wasn't like that at home.

She was the church's scribe for many years and led the small church group to which my parents belonged. In our house, we never skipped Bible study. I didn't like the prayer circle we had each night. Today I am still not a big fan of praying aloud or in a group — even when I am not the one praying. Praying in a group always makes me recall what Bible study was like in my childhood home.

Unfortunately, my mother's perfect image, be it spiritual or social, was nothing other than a mask. And we, as her daughters, definitely formed part of her mask. The pressure was on us to achieve and perform and keep this mask intact.

Allow me now to tell you the story behind the mask. We were three sisters, of which I was in the middle. My eldest sister is just more than eleven years older than me, and my younger sister is just eighteen months younger. My dad was forty-nine years old when I was born, and my mum thirty-nine. They differ in age by almost precisely ten years. My father worked as a clerk on the mine and, when I was about four years old, my father was in a motorcycle accident that cost him most of the movement in his right arm. So he retired early, which meant that he lost his housing benefit, and my parents became first-time homeowners while I was in primary school.

Now that I am married with children of my own to take care of, I can understand that my parents did not have it easy. They must have been under extreme financial pressure: three daughters, early retirement, a disability, new homeowners and a daughter at university. I believe that my mother's mask was her way of escaping and dealing with her less-than-glamorous reality. I also think that she used her mask to hide her pain. She was a strong and resourceful woman; no one could see her as anything other than being strong and in control.

I learned from working with Therapist that there are a few normal responses or ways to address problems in a relationship:

You can get angry or upset. You can scream and throw your toys around and say things that you will probably regret later on.

You can ignore them and go on with your life as if these problems are not there. Even if that means ending the relationship and excluding that person from your life.

You can also ignore them and try to solve the relationship by yourself. Perhaps by giving more of yourself or changing yourself in the way you think will solve your relationship's problems.

You can communicate and work through them together to solve them.

I feel my typical response to issues is one of ignoring them. I can also see that this hasn't always been the case. My mum would often be sick, but she would generally be fighting with my younger sister or me — mostly with me — when she felt well enough and was not in her room. I think my younger sister already figured out that the best thing to do was ignore our mum and withdraw herself from the situation. When my mum's attention was on me, then there couldn't be any fighting with her.

I wasn't that fast a learner; for years, I'd try to fight back. Depending on how "disrespectful" I got or how much I overstepped invisible boundaries, the screaming and shouting would turn into hitting and sometimes even in my mum locking me out of the house for hours until I behaved myself again.

During therapy, I wondered why I did not simply go to one of our next-door neighbours when my mum locked me out of the house. She was concerned about her public image, and something like that might have helped both my sister and me. But I never did. I think I was too afraid of her. Or, perhaps I didn't want people to know that I didn't have a good relationship with my mum? As I got older, I learned to tell my mother what I believed she wanted to hear, even if that meant lying. I would then retreat to my room, usually in tears, as soon as possible.

One afternoon in Grade Twelve, my mum and dad cornered me. My mum wanted to know about the rumours she had heard about my husband being my boyfriend then. My dad formed part of this conversation to support my mum while talking to her errant daughter, but he didn't say anything himself.

My mum started accusing me of being a whore and said that I would never finish school if I continued to see my boyfriend. I was in a relationship with my husband at that stage, but I dismissed everything. I lied to my parents. I lied to my parents a great deal and for many years. I denied my relationship with and my love for my husband on numerous occasions. Of all the things I lied about, those are the deceits by which I feel most hurt. That same afternoon I decided to quit my first diet. I couldn't cope with the diet and my emotions; something had to give.

I want to add that I didn't just finish school. I finished school with seven distinctions and was placed third in the province. I also finished both my undergraduate and honours degrees top of my class. And all of this I did while "whoring" around. Yay for lying and deceiving whores.

Sex was a taboo topic in my childhood home. Even nudity was something shameful. When I was fifteen years old, I developed a nasty yeast infection. It took me three months to work up enough courage to ask my mum for help. That is how uncomfortable it was for me to approach my mother with anything to do with my private parts. I would rather worry for months about a yeast infection that kept spreading down and in-between my thighs, itching so incredibly bad that I could barely sleep, rather than talk to my mum. My parents did not teach me anything about sex — except that pre-marital sex and divorce were sins. Oh, and my mum taught me how to wash out blood from stained underwear and that I should never discuss my bleeding with my dad. Everything else I learned, I learned from school.

An assignment in one of Therapist's courses was to write a letter from your mother to yourself with the message regarding sex that she taught you. Even if she didn't tell you anything, what was it that her not telling you taught you? Then you were to write another letter from you to your daughter(s) telling her/them everything you'd like her/them to know about sex. I didn't feel like doing this assignment. After the third time this assignment popped up, I thought, let me do this silly assignment before getting it a fourth time. Now I believe that these letters are something every mum, even every dad, should read.

Below is the letter that I wrote to myself as if it came from my mum. In this letter, I verbalise what her not telling me and not wanting to talk about sex taught me:

* * *

Sex is something about which you should feel shameful. It is not something that you should talk about, not even in a private conversation. Even the word "sex" is a swear word. All thoughts about sex are dirty and do not belong in good and respectable girls' minds. It is your responsibility to keep your developing body hidden and private. Nobody may know what is happening — even and especially not when you start menstruating. Sex is ugly and dirty. Puberty is ugly and dirty. We don't talk about these things. Not even to your father.

Only loose girls or girls who don't care about their future get involved in relationships. Boys are only interested in sex and will cause you to become pregnant. Now is not the time of your life to get involved with anyone. There will be time for that when you are much older.

* * *

This was the letter I wrote from myself to my daughters:

* * *

Mamma loves you both so very much. All I want is for you to live a fulfilling life and for you to love in abundance without any bounds or limits.

I want you to know precisely how your bodies work and that your bodies are extraordinary. I want you to understand how your bodies develop to prepare for motherhood one day, how pregnancy works, as well as breastfeeding. I also want you to be able to enjoy your bodies. I have so much information and wisdom that I long to pass down to you, and I will do so as time passes. For now, I want you never to hesitate to ask me anything or to come and talk to me.

I never want you to feel uncomfortable when discussing sex. It should be a natural topic for you. Sex is fantastic, but it is also not everything. It is essential to wait for the right person and look forward to meeting this right person. I wish you all the stars in your eyes, feelings of being in love, and butterflies in your stomachs. But I also desire emotional maturity, a clear head, and the insight to make good choices and enter into good and healthy relationships for you. It is essential to work on a good and stable relationship first — a strong foundation — before taking that relationship to a sexual level. Sex is not something to be given out freely or quickly; it is unique and meant for a deserving person. Please don't make it common or cheap.

One day, when you do decide to have sex, my wish is that you will enjoy it for everything it has to offer. I hope you will be able to commit your whole self to it and that the men in your lives will treat you as queens because you deserve nothing less. I hope that you will never stop experimenting, learning, or enjoying. I hope that sex will be the crowning glory of an already beautiful relationship.

* * *

I wrote my letter to my daughters to include the messages I wished I had received when I was a teenager. If I had to use a metaphor to describe the relationship that I had with my mother, I would compare it to a failing marriage. A failing marriage where one party is aware that everything is not fine yet wants people to see them as very happily married. The other party is oblivious to any problems and believes that everything is fine.

I didn't want people to know that I did not have the perfect relationship with my mum. Everyone else's relationships with their mums always seemed so good and happy. On Mother's Day, social media would explode with tributes to mothers. I'd often hear about friends' coffee dates with their mums or their long phone calls. I felt ashamed that our relationship wasn't good and as if the problem was somehow with me. I was also scared that if people knew, then I would have to explain what our relationship was genuinely like — and I wasn't ready for that. I never even wanted to talk to my mum on the phone. When my husband and I visited our hometown, I didn't want to see my mum. When we did visit, our visit was purely out of obligation.

I kept up the facade when talking about my mother to others. I would hang items of hers in our house or decorate our living spaces with something she used to own or had presented me with, like the letter and photograph I had framed. I continued doing this after she passed away. I wanted that perfect relationship so much, even if it meant not telling the truth or if there was no chance of our relationship ever recovering.

We barely started touching the subject of my relationship with my mother in therapy when I needed to go for an operation. The week following my procedure, I had to rest in bed to recover. Lying in bed gave me lots of time to think, and the one thing that consistently popped into my mind and bothered me was that framed photograph and letter hanging in my kitchen. For the first time, I felt an overwhelming urge to remove it. I didn't want to see it, or at the very least, see it less often. I especially didn't want others to see it when they walked into our house.

The first post-operation day that I could get around a bit easier, I got out a ladder and moved that photograph myself. I moved it to a part of my house where I hardly ever see it now. In its place, I hung a beautiful picture of a donkey. My donkey picture has a symbolic meaning and reminds me to remain a humble servant — to serve with love, both God and the people around me. It reminds me not to become too arrogant or overly confident in my abilities — especially in my power to maintain my weight loss.

I drew multiple images of things I felt ashamed of in my self-and-shame-portrait — shame introduced into my life by mostly my mum. Therapist worded it rather well at some stage. He said that if we could take all that shame and weigh it, it would weigh eighty kilograms. While

I had physically lost that weight, I still needed to lose the mental weight to prevent myself from regaining the physical weight.

Gambling

During my first live interview, the interviewer asked, "Where were you born?"

"In Rustenburg," I said, "I grew up in Rustenburg as well. I only left there when I went to university."

Making a very logical connection with the knowledge that there was not much to do in Rustenburg in the 1980s and 1990s, she asked: "Did you go to Sun City a lot growing up?"

I don't think she has any idea what a hurtful "Yes" that was for me to answer.

When I went to Grade One, my older sister was in her final school year, Grade Twelve. She finished school and started university in the year that I went to Grade Two.

University was costly — it still is. Circumstances, as they were, with my mother not working, my father who had just started early retirement and two young girls to cloth and feed, already stretched momentary funds in my childhood home to the max. My parents took loans and had credit cards to pay for other credit cards. "There isn't enough money!" was a phrase I heard a lot growing up. There wasn't even enough money for us for school fees at one stage. I won some cash in a drawing competition the previous year, and my parents used that to pay for schooling for my sister and me that year.

My first recall of my parent's gambling was from around the beginning of my Grade Two year when I was seven years old. I remember that time because my older sister was already staying at her university residence. It was just my younger sister and me still in the nest. In the beginning, gambling happened only on weekend evenings. We would travel to Sun City for my parents to gamble. My mum used to tell us that they are trying to get enough money for my sister's tuition fees or books or residence fees — there was always a perfect reason. I think it was more my mum who was the actual gambler, but because my mum was scared to drive out to Sun City by herself, all of us had to tag along.

My younger sister and I were still underage, and as a result, we were not allowed to enter the casino area. We had to occupy ourselves just outside of the casino area. I am not sure if there was a play area in those days; if there was, we never saw it. Sometimes we would travel to Carnival City and gamble there. They did have a play area that we could use. Thus I am not sure what the problem was at Sun City. Perhaps there were no fees for using Carnival City's play area, and Sun City's did? I did not understand it then, nor can I remember why our parents did not leave us in a play area.

We kept ourselves busy playing on the benches all along the casino area's outside perimeter. Something we loved doing was picking up discarded scratch cards and scratching them to reveal their prizes. Sometimes we won something ourselves. The bingo area was also a lot of fun, and we'd sit on the outside listening to the operator calling out all the numbers. I would also bring some books to read along as I was already a keen reader. We'd often try to spot our parents and then move to a new bench closer to them.

I do not recall having to keep ourselves entertained while my parents were gambling as a traumatic experience. We saw it as being an outing. Sometimes my parents would even buy us ice cream — there was a small shop selling the most amazing bright blue bubblegum ice cream that I loved.

If I think back to this now, I can see how it was wrong, but it did not feel odd about it back then. As a seven-year-old girl, I knew the casino area at Sun City like the back of my hand. My youngest daughter is turning seven this year. I cannot even imagine leaving her anywhere by herself at this stage, let alone with a younger sister to look after.

If either of us got tired, I would try to get my mum or dad's attention. My dad would then take us to our car and let us sleep there. He would leave us there to go back and continue gambling. Later on, my parents got clever and just drove later at night to go gambling, so we would already be asleep in the car by the time we got to Sun City. It was about an hour's drive from where we stayed.

As we got older, from about age thirteen, and when my parents thought it was "safe" to do so, they started leaving us home alone at night. They would wait until we were asleep and then drive off. They didn't communicate this to us. I often woke up realising that our house was empty — no parents. They always returned during the early hours of the morning, had an hour or two's sleep before my dad would get up to take us to school. I am pretty sure they'd take a morning nap then while we were at school.

Even with all the gambling, riches never entered our home. We were always poor. We always had too much debt. There was never money for anything. To this day, still, I'm not too fond of debt. For my entire life, I've tried not to loan money. Where I had no choice, like for a home bond, I would always try to pay it back asap. Basic rule — if I cannot afford to pay for it in cash, then I do not buy it.

When it was time for me to go to university, I said that I would not go if I needed to borrow money. I started searching for a bursary from the last quarter of my Grade Eleven year. I applied everywhere. And I mean everywhere. A private company awarded me a bursary during the middle of Grade Twelve. It was not a full bursary, but enough for my parents to not need to go gambling to subsidise my university costs. I did not want to become another excuse for their gambling problem, although I suspect they often did use it as an excuse. I subsidised my university fees' outstanding portion with performance bursaries.

My parents' gambling had a considerable effect on my life: it is the reason for my aversion to debt, the immense responsibility I felt towards my younger sister, and my ability to fend for myself. Extreme independence — I never wanted to need anyone's help.

I am not sure if my parents stopped gambling when I left home, as I never returned home for long enough to find out. Except maybe for university holidays, but then I didn't notice anything.

What I do notice and acknowledge now is the amount of similarities between myself and my mum. There are so many of her hobbies that I also enjoy. I also have a fear of driving. And I also love gambling …!

For one of our first-year residence socials, we went gambling with one of the male residences on campus. That night I realised just how much fun gambling could be. It is still something I enjoy doing now and again. Still, I am meticulous in setting clear boundaries — only for a specific time and only for a certain amount of money. I know that I can quickly think of myself as not being enough or never having enough, and I also know how deep this rabbit hole can go — being sucked into it is not something I wish to happen.

My Fear Of Driving

I find it very interesting how seemingly unrelated things turn out to be related.

I am afraid of driving, and I am hugely ashamed of admitting it. I am okay with driving when I am familiar with the area, but I become anxious when I need to go out on the freeway or any unfamiliar path.

I usually manage this fear by avoidance. I work from home. When I do travel to our offices, I take the train. Luckily our offices are within walking distance from the train station. When I cannot use public transport, I'll ask my husband if he can take me. My fear of driving is so intense that if I cannot make a plan that does not require me not to drive, I'll quite simply not go.

For the record, I want to state: I can drive. My fear of driving is not an ability problem; it is an anxiety problem. Before starting therapy, I've successfully avoided the driver's seat in situations that cause me anxiety for at least seven years. But while being on my therapy journey, I had a wish that did require driving on the freeway again.

All my therapy sessions up to September 2020 were online. My sessions were online because of the Covid lockdown and Therapist's office being a fifty-minute freeway drive away. My wish was to go for an in-person session at least once. So I asked my husband if he would be willing to take me — being the loving husband he is, he agreed. I was delighted and looking forward to meeting the person that had been helping me for so many months in the flesh. When booking my session, I excitedly selected the in-person option.

The evening before my session, when Therapist confirmed the address with me, I mentioned that he would also be meeting my husband in person the next day. I then noted my aversion to driving and that, as much as I wish it were not the case, I am my mother's daughter when it comes to driving as she also disliked it. Therapist did not respond then, but he revealed a fascinating piece of information to me during our session the next day. He said that being anxious about driving is very common among his clients. For many of his clients, driving to his offices by themselves was a milestone they hope to reach. He believed that my fear of driving was related to the other issues we'd been addressing up to then.

I was stunned! I've always thought that I simply didn't like driving. My mum hardly ever got behind the steering wheel; she would always ask my dad to take her wherever she wanted to be. Thus, when Therapist suggested that I feared driving and that this fear was related to my other problems, I did not believe him. I told him that it did not make sense to me and that I thought he was wrong. He gave me a look that said: "Give it some time; you'll come around eventually."

It did not take me long to come around.

The team that I work in had finished a big project, and we had a team celebration planned a few weeks after my session. The planned party was a team lunch at an off-site location — about forty-five minutes drive away from my home — out on the freeway!

I had the following dilemma: I couldn't take the train, my husband could not take me there as it was during office hours and not going was not an option as I'd already RSVP-ed. Also, I wanted to go as I haven't seen the rest of my team for the entire duration of the lockdown. I was looking forward to this celebration so much. Considering my dilemma, if I were to go, I had no other option but to drive myself there.

The Monday afternoon before our celebration, after checking the route probably thirty times on Google maps for any "problem areas" and planning my outfit to show the least amount of sweat, I realised that my behaviour was not at all typical. I was busy having a panic attack, and the drive was still days away!

I didn't just dislike driving; I was indeed anxious about it. Yes, I can plan as far as possible not to find myself in that situation again. But certainly, as a thirty-nine-year-old adult, I should have the confidence to drive myself to a work function? It was the silliest situation ever. I felt that I was stupid. I want to be a confident, independent woman, but I fear getting behind the steering wheel?

Therapist's response to my confession that he was correct and that I did have driving anxiety was luckily not: "I told you so." He said that a big reason for me going to therapy was to learn self-authority over all aspects of my life — like my eating, screaming, and driving — instead of applying my typical reaction- and emotion-based control.

I did face my fear and drove myself to our work function, but it was not pretty. I was in tears for most of the way there, and I've probably upset a lot of other drivers with my slow driving. But I made it safely there and back — and that was all that mattered — that and the fact that I took a first step to facing my fear instead of avoiding it and not going.

Therapist and I never got around to discussing my fear in-depth, but I did some own therapy while writing this book to understand its origin. Two accidents that affected my life were my dad's motorcycle accident in which he lost the use of his right arm and an accident my grandmother and I were involved in when I was very young. But it is not in those accidents where I saw how my problem started.

Because my mum was afraid, she told us each time before entering a car that we should remember that a vehicle was a murder weapon. She expected us to treat a car as something that can harm and kill. My mum also insisted that anyone outside of our family had to sign a non-disclaimer before driving with us — I kid you not! We were ashamed of offering lifts to anyone. My mother had brainwashed me to believe that driving was something to fear.

My fear of driving was initially for any driving, not just driving on unfamiliar roads. I never climbed in behind the steering wheel again after getting my driver's license. I passed my driving test two days before leaving for university. But after my driving test, I resigned from steering until just before I married — which was almost four years later.

A month before getting married, I purchased my first car and bumped it on the first day I drove it — that did not help! I stuck with only commuting to work and back. Over time I became familiar with driving in our area. As a mum of four children, I've needed to make peace with driving within at least five kilometres of our home as I am required to do it all the time.

I am still working on my fear of driving on the freeway and unfamiliar roads. My husband now fears that once I have this driving thing sorted, I will take all my clothes and hit the road. As if I will ever do that, I will take my earrings as well!

Losing Our First Baby

I was in pain. I didn't think that it would hurt so much. Yet, there I was in the doctor's rooms, watching the near-empty sonar screen and feeling like someone stabbed something right through my heart. When the doctor told me that there was nothing more he could do for us, I felt defeated. No, it cannot be. Surely there must be one more thing that we can try? Anything? I will try anything. Just give me something to try. I'd been so good over the previous two days; how could this have happened? To give up? To not have even a little bit of hope left?

It was as if the air had suddenly become very thin, and I was struggling to breathe. I just cried. It felt like such a nonsensical thing to do. Crying was not going to solve anything. It was not going to bring our baby back. Was crying the only option that remained? Such a hopeless action. Would that somehow make me hurt less? It felt like it was making me hurt more.

Yet, I continued crying: while my husband was booking us a hospital room at the reception, on the way walking to the hospital room, while lying in bed waiting for the procedure to remove the remains of our baby. It was the only proof that I was pregnant, and now that only proof is taken away from me as well. Was the fetus in one of the blood clots I held in my hand that morning? Did I flush our baby down the toilet?

For nine glorious weeks I grew in excitement, and then our baby, my body or faith, decided to halt that excitement. Losing our baby is not what I wanted. Why cry over a baby that had hardly existed in the first place? Especially when it is so easy to remove any evidence of that existence. It is a simple procedure, and then you are clean and rid of the hope you had carried in your heart. Clean physically, but a mess emotionally. Hope had died — and nothing could've caused me more pain than that.

* * *

My husband and I married when we were twenty-three. That was a young age to marry, and we were the first couple in our peer group to do so. We had to figure out many things ourselves and couldn't call on friends' help or experience.

One of the things customarily discussed before marriage is how many children you'd like to have — well, that is what I've heard is the norm. My husband grew up in a family with two sons, and I grew up in a family with three daughters. We didn't know how many children we'd like to have as a couple. We entered our marriage, deciding to start with one child and then take it from there. If it goes well, we will have more. If we considered one child was enough, we would stop there. We thought this was a good plan.

I wonder if all women have a deep longing to become mothers? Is this deep desire perhaps something built into human DNA by default? I know now that I do not have a natural mothering instinct or nurturing personality; thus, I am unsure how 'the wish to reproduce' initiated in my thoughts. Nonetheless, after three years of marriage, I had a strong urge to become a mum.

When we decided the time was right, I believed the first natural step was to go off my oral contraception. After about two months, I already had a positive pregnancy test — we were elated. But I had never been to a gynaecologist and didn't even know of a good one. I wasn't expecting to fall pregnant so soon and thought it would take many months to find a gynaecologist who suited me.

We shared this news with just our immediate families. Because we were so inexperienced at the whole pregnancy thing, we tried to do everything by the book. Book knowledge dictates that you wait till at least twelve weeks before going share crazy with your happy news.

In retrospect, I think this is a terrible idea. When something does go wrong before twelve weeks, and you have hardly shared your announcement, you have no one to support you. And nobody understands your grief as no one got excited with you.

On a Tuesday, about four weeks after our positive pregnancy test, I started spot bleeding. We had already nicknamed our baby "Baby Bummy" by then. My husband ordered a little "Devil Ducky" bath toy for our baby; he thought it was adorable — it was.

We didn't know what to make of this bleeding. I still didn't have a gynaecologist by then, so we went back to our books. Bleeding could be a sign of many things. We tried not to be too worried, but by the following morning, the bleeding was worse, and suddenly, I really needed to find a gynaecologist. We walked into our nearest hospital's reception area and down the stairs to the consulting rooms that Wednesday morning in our search for a gynaecologist. We turned left into the first corridor where the doctor's rooms were, and the first office on our left happened to be that of a gynaecologist. We decided, right then and there as we were standing outside of that office door, that we would go to this one and change later on if we needed to. After fourteen years, five pregnancies and four children, I am still going to the same doctor.

We explained our situation to the receptionist. She instructed us to sit and wait for a gap in the doctor's schedule. I thought we would wait for the entire day, but the doctor could see us quite soon. For our first sonar, we saw a perfect baby. Stubs for arms and legs, a big head, measuring almost nine weeks already. Almost at the magical twelve weeks where we could share our news. But the doctor couldn't find a heartbeat. He booked me off from work and instructed me to rest for a few days. We scheduled another appointment for a week later. Our doctor still hoped for a favourable outcome.

That Wednesday evening, we had a weekly meeting with our church friends. My husband broke the news to them like this: "We have some good news. We are expecting, but there are some complications. Mart-Mari started bleeding, and this morning at our first sonar, there was no heartbeat. There should be a heartbeat by now, but the doctor is still hopeful. We have another sonar scheduled for next week."

The bad news with good news. Never an opportunity for our friends to be happy for us.

God does not always answer prayers in the way you want Him to. My hope faded as I continued bleeding even more the next day and into the Friday. When I started passing clots by the Friday morning, all my remaining hope had left me. We contacted our doctor. After a quick visit to the rooms for another sonar, he instructed us to go straight to hospital reception to book a bed for a D&C. Our doctor wanted to clean all foetal matter from the uterus as a precaution.

I could not utter a word sitting there in the hospital reception while my husband was busy booking my hospital bed. The reality of the situation was just too grim. I had miscarried my first pregnancy at just short of nine weeks. My heart had never been more broken.

One thing I remember vividly from lying in my bed while waiting for the D&C was all the hair that I was losing. My hair was still long then, and it was falling out in clumps. It was the weirdest thing. I am not sure if all the stress caused that to happen. I discovered later that I would shed hair for weeks after each child's birth. So maybe it is just a regular occurrence from giving birth?

Later that afternoon, my doctor came to sign me out to go home during his ward rounds. There was a cricket game about to start that I wanted to watch. I love cricket. I joked and told my doctor that he needs to sign me out soon so I could still catch the game in the comfort of my own home. It was my way of trying to make something light of an already very sombre mood and situation. I didn't even watch the game when I got home. It was suddenly not crucial to me anymore. Nothing else was important anymore.

I was booked off work for the following Monday and Tuesday, but thinking that I was okay, I went back to work the Monday already. Going back to work so soon was not a good idea. The problem wasn't that everyone was asking me questions about what happened. The previous week I'd already explained the situation to my boss. He was kind enough to inform my colleagues and make them aware of what had happened.

But sitting there at my desk, it felt like everyone was staring at me and feeling sorry for me. I was still feeling sorry for myself and had not taken the time to deal with things either. My attention was not on my work. It felt impossible to sit and work as if nothing had happened — even when everyone respected my privacy and didn't ask questions.

I was so sad. I thought I had already cried out all my tears that weekend, but clearly, I had not. Feeling the tears building, I got up, packed my things, and proceeded straight out of there. My boss was outside on his way in, he still tried to grab my shoulder to get my attention and possibly a word in, but I brushed him off — I was already crying by then. He messaged me later to tell me to take as much time as I needed.

I do not understand how one could be so emotional over a baby who had never really lived. Perhaps it is because a dream died? We were excited and looking forward to becoming parents.

Selective perception is a bitch. Suddenly there were pregnant women everywhere I went. A friend had her baby about a week after my miscarriage. Another friend phoned me that week to tell me that she was expecting. I told her then that I had also been pregnant but had miscarried. Crappy news indeed to share in response to her good news.

I realise that a miscarriage is not uncommon and that it happens to thousands of women each year, but it hurts so much. People's well-intended words also didn't help.

"At least you were not that far along yet."

"You can always try again."

"You are still young."

"There might have been something wrong with the baby. Miscarrying is better than giving birth to a baby with problems."

"This is God's plan."

Our doctor said we could try for a second pregnancy as soon as I felt up to it. He said that my body was ready and wanted to be pregnant and that he had a high success ratio of women falling pregnant immediately after a miscarriage. He was not wrong. I fell pregnant again in the month immediately following my miscarriage, before even getting my next period. There was no last date of menstruation for that pregnancy. This time we told everyone we wanted to tell our good news as soon as we could. It felt amazing being able to share that news.

Our second pregnancy made us the proud parents of a wonderful son, but it also caused me to gain a tremendous amount of weight. The most weight I have ever put on with any of my pregnancies. I was very hard on myself after the miscarriage. I spent hours Googling and reading about what I could have done to prevent that miscarriage. I was determined not to lose another pregnancy. I spared no effort. If I were to lose another pregnancy, it would not be due to any wrongdoing on my part. So I ate. I ate, and I ate, and I ate. Eating away my grief and all my imperfections — yet never being good enough.

I also made a big decision that would affect the rest of my life. Babies are a blessing. Our initial approach of having one child and seeing how it goes thing was nonsense. I wanted to have as many children as I could afford and as my health would allow.

My Father's Death

Friday, 11 April 2003, was the day of my graduation. It was also the last day that I spent any significant time with my father while still alive.

I saw myself as having had a reasonably good relationship with my dad. He was always the one who would drop us off in the mornings for school and come to pick us up in the afternoons. Sometimes he would stop by the small 'fish and slap chips' cafe that smelled of vinegar on the way home to buy us something nice to eat. We would always eat in the car, so my mum wouldn't find out. My dad also had a great sense of humour and could tell the funniest jokes. He also never shouted at me, nor did he ever hit me.

It was my dad's seventieth birthday on the 24'th of April. My younger sister and I organised an ice cream cake for him for his birthday. When I phoned him that day, he said he wasn't feeling well. That already raised concerns for me as my dad never complained about not feeling well. It was always my mum who was the one not feeling well.

On the Saturday after my dad's seventieth birthday, my dad was admitted to the hospital. Later the following afternoon, my mum phoned me to let me know that she thought it would be a good idea to drive through if I still wanted to see my dad alive. I didn't have a car then. I didn't need one as I stayed in my university residence and could walk everywhere I needed to be. My husband, who was then still my secret boyfriend, offered me a lift, and we drove straight to the hospital. By the time I got there, my dad's body had already started shutting down. He had somehow contracted Hepatitis, and his organs failed one after the other. My dad passed away just after midnight in the early hours of the morning on the 28'th of April 2003.

What happened during the rest of that week is a haze to me. I cannot remember if my boyfriend came to stay overnight at my childhood home or went to his parental house. I know he went back on Monday morning, as he had to be at work. I had university assignments that were due that week. I was working on those tasks when I answered my mother's call. Some of those projects were still unfinished. But somehow, my boyfriend figured out how to submit the work that was due that week. A friend packed some clothes for me from my residence room, which made it to me without me orchestrating it. If you experience intense emotional hurt, your mind goes on some form of auto-pilot. Like you are living, but you are not recording.

I know that my dad's death was a massive shock and that I spent days mourning his passing. He was our buffer to dealing with my mum. I did not know how to do that independently, and I never realised that I didn't until he was no longer there. He left a big void behind, and I regret him not ever getting to know me as an adult.

Unpacking My Closet

I am a visual person; I think in pictures. I also draw illustrations for myself when I am trying to understand something. I did Art as a subject up until Grade Twelve. I love drawing. I wish I could spend more time with my drawing book and pencils.

Sometimes I dream of something that feels so vivid and real. It is just my mind trying to make sense of things. I call these dreams visions, but I am not sure if that is the right word. Perhaps they are just normal dreams that I remember well?

The first of these "visions" that I shared with Therapist was of me standing with my back against a closed closet. I needed to keep the closet closed — it was just too full. This closet contained all the guilt, shame, and hurt I carried with me for years.

I was trying to keep the contents of it hidden by pressing against the barely closing doors with my back. My favourite way of dealing with issues had become to shove them away in my closet and pretend that they do not exist. However, over time these issues started rotting and turning toxic. They became too much, and they made me an unhealthy person.

Therapist instructed me, "Imagine yourself stepping away from the closet and allowing all its contents to fall out on the floor. Then imagine yourself standing in the middle of this mess. How does that make you feel?"

"It makes me feel exposed. I have to resist the urge to start picking up and packing the mess away," I replied.

"Don't start cleaning just yet. Just stand there for a bit. Now imagine someone walking in on you while you are standing in the middle of the mess. Who would walk in on you?" Therapist asked.

"I think the most likely person to walk in on a scenario like this would be my eldest son."

Therapist enquired further, "Imagine that he does discover you standing in the middle of this mess. What would he think of his mum? What would his reaction be?"

"He'd probably think I was ridiculous. He might even try to help me clean up," I replied.

"Who else might walk in on you?" Therapist asked, continuing on this line of exposing my shame to people in my life that are close to me.

Thinking of the one person in my life that means the most to me, I replied, "My husband might walk in on me."

"And what would his reaction be?"

"He would most likely just give me a hug."

We continued along with this vision with more and more people walking in on this mess until Therapist stated, "Can you see that none of the people you imagined walking in on your mess of shame judged you?"

Therapist was right. Not once did I answer along the line of "He is going to see that ... and then he is going to storm out and leave me by myself." That is what I feared would happen, if I dared reveal any of my secrets. I feared that I would be judged, in trouble, or reprimanded. Maybe if I played this vision out as a teenager, I would have responded along that line.

But, at that stage of my life, I could see that the people I held close were not out to judge me.

Therapist was, however, not one of them. He was my therapist and, essentially, still a stranger to me. Yet, his next question was one I had feared even before deciding to share this vision with him. I decided to share this vision with him because of one item in my closet that screamed at me.

When I opened the cupboard to catch a quick peek inside, it was this item that stood out among all of the others. More than me causing my mum a tremendous amount of pain and suffering. More than pre-marital sex. More than not giving my dad the eulogy that he deserved. More than all the lying and deceiving. More than denying my love for my husband. More than all the fat that I carried with me or the years of failed dieting attempts. More than my stretch marks and excess skin. More than feeling that I was a failed Christian.

Therapist asked me, "When you look at all the items lying around you on the floor, is there one that stands out to you? If there is, which one is it?"

Goodness! I decided to share this vision because of this item, and suddenly I wanted to chicken out. I started crying inconsolably, and through my devastated sobbing I tried to reply.

"The one item on the floor that stands out most to me is that I feel so incredibly relieved, happy even, that my mum passed away."

Saying that I felt relieved because my mum was not alive anymore was a horrible thing to admit. For sure, nobody else can feel this way about their biological mother? My parents provided me with a stable home. I had a roof over my head and food to eat. I was able to attend school and even university. I am so privileged. At the very least, I could feel indifferent about my mum passing away, but no — I felt relieved.

Do you know those times in your life when you feel undeserving? When someone goes through a massive amount of effort for you, and you think that a simple "Thank you" cannot come close to expressing your gratitude. Or when you were on your worst behaviour, and someone treated you as if it had never happened. Or when someone does something for you knowing that you will not be able to repay them — yet they still do it.

What Therapist said next, I was not expecting at all. I expected him to judge me. Perhaps reply along the lines of: "Yes, you are a horrible daughter." But this is not what he did. Instead, he said, "Yes, I am also happy and relieved about that."

Speechless! Those who know me well will know that I am rarely speechless.

Of all the things Therapist has ever said to me, this reply meant the most to me. This reply made me feel like I could tell him anything without fearing judgement.

Speaking one's mind is such an important thing to do in therapy. Therapy had to be a place where I could stop pretending to be perfect and have everything under control. Where I could just be "me". Whatever "me" meant and regardless of how scary and cruel "me" was.

My mother's death was not like my father's at all. When my older sister phoned me to let me know that my mother passed away, I was already cold towards the news. I was at a cash register in a nursery buying Lavender plants. I felt sorry for the person assisting me as she appeared more shocked with the news than I was. Those Lavender plants never grew, and perhaps that is a good thing as they would've been a constant reminder to me of my reaction that day.

The last dispute I remember having with my mum was over me attending her funeral. Yes, she argued with me over me attending her funeral even before she passed away. A few days before our fight my uncle, my mum's brother, phoned me.

"You know that your mum is very sick, right? You and your sister should look after her better and show more interest."

"Well, she has always been sick. I do not know when to take her seriously and when not to. Most of the time, I am sure she is making things up for attention," I replied.

"Well, she is genuinely sick this time," my uncle insisted.

A day or so later, my mum phoned me, "I hear you say that I am making things up again?"

I replied, "I am sorry, but I genuinely do not know when you are sick or when you are only pretending to be. It is always the same story; It has always been the same story! You cry wolf until everyone feels sorry for you, and you can get what you want."

"But what else do I have to do to get you guys to come and visit and to bring my grandchildren to visit. They are growing up without me. One of these days, your only remaining option would be to 'visit' me at my funeral."

"That is if we will attend your funeral," I said.

I did drive through to Rustenburg to help my older sister pack up my mum's home and belongings. I helped my sister because she needed the help and did not deserve to do it solo. I also wondered and found it strange at the time as my younger sister wanted nothing from my mum and hardly stayed to help — I understand her behaviour now. I did not want to do a eulogy at my mum's funeral. My sister and my mum's minister did ask me to, but I refused, using my dad's eulogy as an excuse. But that was not the reason.

Therapist feels that one day I would mourn my mum's death. Perhaps that will be one day when I am watching a movie? I genuinely do not know if I ever will or how that will come about. I sympathise with my mum's situation, and I understand that she must have been under a lot of pressure. She was a remarkable woman: so strong and talented. But too much water has passed underneath the bridge. I am not sure if the coldness I have in my heart will ever disappear.

The Exercise I Could Not Do

I sucked at therapy. I know I sometimes make it sound like working through therapy naturally came to me, but it didn't. It was hard work. I was fortunate to have a natural, comfortable connection with Therapist. This connection was primarily due to his own doing and the person he is.

I took all of the exercises and assignments I received during therapy seriously. I didn't always want to do them, but I knew that each one had a purpose. Therapist didn't hand them out just for the sake of giving me something to do. I was perfectly capable of keeping myself busy.

I also wanted him to "mark" my work and tell me if I am doing okay at therapy or not. He never did. He was far too clever to fall for those tricks. In retrospect, it was such a silly thing to want him to do, but I felt like I was trying so hard yet still failing. I needed the reassurance that I was doing okay — or I thought that I did.

Only after my therapy sessions concluded did I see what I was doing. It took another friend of mine to make me see it. I was writing the piece on how my sessions with Therapist started. The direct speech was tricky to write. English is not my first language, and I was unsure if I was writing the complex dialogue correctly. I sent my friend the first draft asking her specifically to look at the direct speech. On reading it, she invited me over to discuss it. After our discussion, which never got to the correct grammatical usage of direct speech, I asked her, "So do you think I got the dialogue parts right?"

"Ah, you are going back into your school girl mode again. You want me to mark your grammar and give you a gold star. I am not going to do that," she replied. Therapist had said something very similar to me as well before.

Schoolgirl mode? What schoolgirl mode? Why did I not know about this schoolgirl mode?

I have this natural tendency to want to please and perform. I used to think this was a good thing. Perhaps in some ways, it is, but in most ways, it is not.

"Anything worth doing is worth doing well."

The above was a mantra by which I would live. When I was younger, I applied it to my school work. As I got older, I used it for everything else. If I enrolled on a course, I would partake fully. Any program. Any relationship. No half measures — ever. It is no wonder that a stranger, like Therapist, made the observation, after just a few months of taking some of his courses, that "It must be so tiring to always be so perfect."

It is not wrong to want to partake fully and try to get the most out of opportunities or even apply yourself fully to whatever you do. I just needed to learn to chill a bit. I did not need to do everything worth doing well. Sometimes I could do something just because it is fun. Or perhaps simply because you want to try it. I used not to try new things because I couldn't see myself doing them well beforehand. I also used to quit challenges if I saw that I would not be able to do it well anymore. Which I think is a big reason why I yo-yo dieted so much.

I directly linked my feelings of worthiness of being loved to my achievements. If I could achieve something, then I would be worthy of love. In my experience, I needed to work for love; love was not something handed out on a silver platter. A problem occurred when, after losing eighty kilograms and working very hard to do that, I still found myself in a position where I did not love myself.

The root of this desire to please and perform comes from my childhood. Growing up, I wanted to make my mum love me. I now know that you cannot make anyone else love you, but then it seemed to me like it was a possibility. I would perform. I would get good marks at school. I would write cards and pick flowers for her in the garden. I was a good child — the perfect child. But nothing I did seemed to work.

Instead of receiving her love, I received my mum's temper in the form of her screaming, shouting and hitting. Yes, I guess one could say that most children of the 1980s and 1990s were yelled at and even smacked. Many adults today, who grew up in that era, attribute their success in life to the discipline they received from their parents.

The problem in my case was that my mum did not discipline me. She would punish me even when I brought home good marks from school. Even if I helped clean the house or stayed in my bedroom every afternoon for the entire afternoon to read. I could not do anything right. My mum would find something to be unhappy about, and then it would be my problem.

Her screaming was a distinct repetitive, illogical lament. I couldn't even reason my way out of it as it made no sense. She would start with an initial hook of something that was not right according to her, and then she would spiral from there, working herself up more and more in the process.

On the days that I did something wrong and needed discipline, it was much worse. Even the slightest misdemeanour and I could end up with bruises I needed to cover up. Luckily I did not have admirable arms or legs, so covering up was not problematic.

What bothers me most is that I seemed to have "inherited" some of my mum's screaming behaviour, specifically towards my husband and children. It is not as bad as I experienced from my mother, but it is the same type of screaming. Most often, this screaming happens when I feel overwhelmed or frustrated, which might have been the case for my mum as well? I am often shocked by my words when I go into that mode. Too familiar! Too scary! I feel ashamed of this behaviour.

As I shared anything with Therapist, I shared this screaming behaviour asking for his help. The exercise he wanted me to try was to imagine myself as a child standing up for myself against my mum. He wanted me to visualise a type of sparring fight with her.

"Imagine yourself at a certain age being trapped in a fight with your mum. What age are you?"

"Okay ... I am fifteen."

"What is your reaction when your mum starts fighting with you?"

"I retreat. I go to my room and close the door. I lie on my bed with my pillow over my ears. I try to ignore my mum's screaming."

"No, you are already at an age where you have become hardened to her fighting. Imagine yourself much younger. What age are you now?"

"Let's try nine years old."

"Okay, what do you do when she starts fighting with you?"

"I cry. I do not know what to do."

"Try screaming back."

"If I scream back, she will hit me."

"Then hit her back."

"I cannot do that!"

"But you have to. That is the only way to defeat a bully. You have to stand up for yourself."

"That is not how I teach my children to fight against a bully. I teach them not to respond to violence with violence. I teach them not to be guilty of the same behaviour."

"You are watching too many Disney movies. You have to teach that nine-year-old how to stand up for herself. Nine years might even be too old; perhaps we should try six or four years old? If we can give power to the four-year-old you, we can give power to the six-year-old, the nine-year-old, the fifteen-year-old, and so on, until we can give back power to the thirty-nine-year-old. You are currently acting out your mother's modelled behaviour because you could never stand up against it yourself as a child. You don't want to become a bully as well."

"Perhaps it is too late? Perhaps I am already a bully?"

I didn't want to suck at therapy. Neither did I want to be a bully. I used to try this exercise early every morning. I even started making a list of all the possible outcomes my fights with my mum could have and the potential solutions. But I always ended up freezing or fleeing. I never managed to see a fight through and win it.

Therapist's suggested exercise to resolve my screaming problem was an exercise that I could not get right. No matter how hard I tried — perhaps I tried too hard? Not even if I imagined myself as a four-year-old — especially not as a four-year-old. I convinced myself that I was forever doomed to be a bully of my children.

One day — after yet another failed attempt — I had a brainwave. I thought, "I might struggle to handle this fight effectively, but maybe I can teach my children and my husband to handle the situation correctly?" With that in mind, that night around the dinner table, I explained the whole story. I then asked them to call me out when they experience this behaviour from me. Not to shout back or to get upset. Just a simple "Mum, you are doing that thing again" will suffice.

Strangely enough, me coming forward with my problem and asking my family's help made me feel as if I was taking some of my power back. That I was not doomed to be a bully after all, which felt good, it felt like I could do something about my current situation while still figuring out how to stand up for myself.

I had further insights into my struggles around performing this exercise one day when Therapist suggested another similar exercise for me to try.

During my fights with my mum, something that would often happen is that she would work herself up into such a state that she would eventually retreat to her room, refusing to come out. My dad, who had a gentle heart and just wanted peace, would then ask me to go and apologise to her.

As Therapist explained, my dad expected me to take responsibility for my feelings and hers. Therapist challenged me to play this scenario back in my mind and then tell my dad to sort it out himself.

I already struggled to fight with my mum. Now Therapist added this challenge to my plate as well. The first thing I told Therapist was that I would never talk back to my dad. I had too much respect for him. He never picked a fight with me, and I had no desire to fight him either.

But I was wrong. On my very first attempt at this challenge, I managed to imagine telling my dad, "No, I will not go and apologise. I did nothing wrong. Sort out your shit!" I could see him being disappointed yet respecting what I had said.

Talking back to my dad made me realise something: as a thirty-nine-year-old adult, I was still scared of my mum. I never had an open communication channel with her either. I did not respect her sufficiently to tell her my truth. I would rather lie and deceive her into believing what I thought she wanted to hear. That is why I found standing up for myself against her, even if it was just in my imagination, so incredibly difficult.

When I hear the unasked opinions of my children now, I love them even more. I am not fond of them talking back, but voicing their feelings and emotions means seeing me as approachable. Perhaps they are not always as respectful as they should be, but we can work on that. It is when they turn silent that I should start worrying.

I wish I could have been the perfect daughter. Perhaps it would have made life so much easier? But I never was, not least when measured against my mother's extremely high standards. I was the lying and deceiving daughter. I was the daughter who never visited enough. I was the disrespectful daughter. I was the daughter who fell in love before finishing my studies.

When Therapist initially pointed out my desire to be perfect, I felt rather insulted. Over time I have come to hate perfectionism. When I see people pretending to be something they are not, putting on a fake persona, pushing their children to be perfect or posting their ideal social media posts and photos, I roll my eyes.

One reason for hating perfectionism might be that I could never be perfect myself and never get my mum's approval? But I think it is more because I have firsthand experience at the shadow persona behind the mask of perfection. Seeing people putting their perfect lives on display makes me feel nauseous. What is the shadow like?

I wish with my entire heart that my mum would have allowed others to see her for who she genuinely was. That she could sometimes have admitted that she also needed help, that her life wasn't perfect, and that her daughters weren't perfect either. Perhaps if she could have received the support she needed, things might have been better for my sister and me? Maybe my younger sister might have been better able to cope with her problems and depression?

My problems with perfectionism are complex. On the one hand, I feel that I should be perfect and do everything perfectly and then everyone will love me. I work for love and approval. On the other hand, I am deeply concerned about the mask of perfectionism and the shadow persona behind such a mask.

I will forever be a work in progress.

I have since changed my mantra: "Do anything worth doing to the best of your ability." Sometimes just having fun is the best of my ability.

I still cannot imagine myself as a four-year-old standing up to my mother. Perhaps I never will, but that doesn't matter. At least my children stand up for themselves against me.

The Motivator's Curse

People often message me with their dreams of being thin. They will say that they have joined a weight loss group, or started a new exercise program or even joined a gym. But they do not want anyone else to know about it yet. They are entrusting their secret to me. They realise they cannot do it by themselves, but they have no one else to turn to for support.

I consider these strangers choosing to entrust me with their big "secret" and hope for something more, to be an incredible privilege. I feel honoured to be thought of as an inspiration enough to share their dreams with me. And when I receive such a message, I feel as if I want to reach out across the internet cable and give them a hug and permission to dream. I have compassion for this secretive behaviour and understand that this behaviour might seem strange to someone that hasn't been in such a position before.

If you have a dream to work on yourself, it is never just about you. Yes, you may be the one with the vision, and you are trying to do it for yourself, but there are always people around you. People close to you might understand your struggles and why you want to try and will support you. Some friends or family might even have the same dream as you and want to try it together. Others might have failed at your goal countless times themselves and can now either be supportive or not of your efforts.

The dynamics around people and their support vary greatly, and I believe this will always be the case. When your dream is fresh and your hope so vulnerable, you feel as if you cannot entrust it with just anyone who may potentially squash it.

Initially, I was very secretive on my journey to losing eighty kilograms. I was very mysterious because I realised that not everyone close to me would be supportive. I was sensitive to my sister's weight and depression problems. If I were to tell her of my new weight loss journey, she would have said something like, "Why do you need to lose weight? I need to lose weight first. Anyway, you are not following a good diet. You have never been able to keep any weight loss off either, so it is just going to be the same story again this time."

My sister would have been right. I was not convinced that I would not fail yet again at losing weight. I had tried and failed so many times before. I was preempting the shame of admitting defeat before even starting. If my sister were to point that out to me, she would have fed my fear at a very fragile stage of my new dream, and she would have crushed the tiny bit of hope that I had of success.

So I chose not to tell anyone besides my husband, my children, and two close friends when I rejoined Weigh-Less. Unfortunately, I picked two friends who were also overweight to be part of my initial support group. After a few weeks of losing consistently, they also wanted to join. Neither of them could see the program through. With their failures came a lack of support for my efforts. The bitterness I perceived from them attempted to pull me down as well. One of them would say that she lost so much better when following diet x and that the diet that I was on was not so good. The other would say that she wasted money on Weigh-Less and then list the things she wanted to buy instead.

In response to their bitterness, I stopped relying on them for support by not sharing my journey with them anymore. I lost two good friends. Having completed my weight loss journey, I am trying to mend things with one of them, but the other I believe is gone for good.

Another friend also started attending the same weight loss group that I went to a few months later. I was delighted to have a buddy for mutual support again. Unfortunately, things didn't work out for her either, and after a few months, she quit the program. Losing weight is hard work and takes a very determined mindset.

When she stopped attending, I also stopped sharing my journey with her. I assumed that things would pan out the same way as my other two friends. I had already lost two friends, and I was determined not to lose another one. But she insisted that I keep sharing my successes and my failures. She continued to be a pillar of support right up to the day that I reached my goal weight, and after that, even when she immigrated. When I achieved my goal weight, she was the first person I messaged. I am indeed very blessed to have someone like her in my life.

Whatever mission we are on in life or dream that we might be pursuing, we all need someone with whom we don't need to pretend. Someone to whom we can say, "I am not coping", when asked, "How are you doing?"

If you start being successful on the way to your goal and others notice your improvement, you find yourself in a challenging position. Suddenly you cannot hide your dreams, wishes, and plans anymore. Whether you like it or not, you will become a motivation to others. Others will approach you for advice and your opinion, especially if your dream had something to do with a physical quality — such as weight — as even strangers quickly notice a positive difference.

For my sister, the weight that I lost was a particularly bitter pill to swallow. She desperately wanted to lose weight. I tried to pull her in on my journey subtly, but she would have none of it. My group leader asked if I would be willing to present at an open meeting in December 2017 — my first invitation of this kind. I shared an advertisement for this talk on my Facebook profile. This advertisement was the first time I had ever shared anything about my weight loss on social media. It was a big thing for me to do, as I still wanted to work on this project in silence. I wasn't ready to share anything yet, and I was still far from my end goal. But I was hoping I could somehow get my sister to come to my talk. My idea backfired. She was upset by my post and decided to block and unfollow me. I didn't know this until her husband talked about it after her suicide the following year in November.

I do not regret sharing my journey publicly, though. I've learned that strength and accountability come from sharing and helping others. I wish to inspire and help others reach their goals as well. I know what it is like on both sides of the dream. I desire to pull others up out of their struggles through my story.

> *"There is a wonderful, almost mystical, law of nature that says three of the things we want most — happiness, freedom, and peace of mind — are always attained when we give them to others. Give it away to get it back."*
> — John Wooden

This desire to share my story and experiences is not uncommon; many people who have been through a life-changing journey themselves wish to do the same. I call this group of people *Motivators*.

Some motivators, like myself, will try to reach out to more people and share their stories to a broader audience through group talks, live events, motivational talks etc. Suddenly their story is not just for their family and friends but also strangers. When sharing my story with strangers, my initial thoughts were that people would hate it, not like me or be cruel. Mostly not the case at all. The audience's intent toward the person sharing their story is to draw inspiration from them. The audience's objective is not to pull down the motivator. They want the motivator to be successful. Of course, the audience would not wish the presenter any harm; it seems like an obvious statement to make. But it is crucial to understand that there are people out there, strange as it may seem, whose intent is to pull those who should motivate them down instead of being inspired by the inspiration they receive.

Most motivators chose to inspire only those within their friend and family circle. Even those who decide to be more public start within those circles. I am not only talking about motivational stories the size of losing eighty kilos; I am referring to all motivational stories — be it as small as going for counseling or trying to learn a new skill. The same principle applies. It is not always the intent of friends and family to pull you up; sometimes, they may want to hinder or prevent your progress or demotivate you enough so you'll become despondent and quit.

My husband has always been my leading supporter. He said right from the onset of each weight loss journey I have been on and the one I lost eighty kilos on, that he would support me no matter what it took.

He would eat what I eat. He would keep an eye on my eating. He was so excited to hear how every week's weigh-in went. When I started running, so did he. We don't run at the same pace, but when we pass each other on the road, we sneak a quick kiss — I think we freak out a few people in these Covid times. He has also lost more than forty kilograms himself through the entire process. This weight loss happened by joining me in my new lifestyle, never by joining Weigh-Less as a proper member himself.

Ultimately, the response to you trying to better your life can be that of support or critique. You have to choose how you respond to critique, especially when the critic tries to hamper your efforts and demotivate you. Sometimes that person will walk away and let you be on their own accord. The problem comes when the critic refuses to cut ties with you themselves. If you wish to avoid further demotivation, you then have to be the one to make the break while still maintaining an olive branch for the one day when they will need you again. Turning your back on people whom you hoped would support you and whom you know needs support themselves is tough to do. I didn't want to lose my friends, but I couldn't continue being friends with them while they were constantly trying to find flaws and weaknesses over which I could stumble. Mostly, I wanted to be there for them for that one day when they decided that perhaps they needed my help after all.

It is even more challenging when the critic is someone in your household or a close family member, and you cannot cut ties with them. Having an unsupportive family member is rarely the case as the closest people to you are usually proud and supportive. However, when the unfortunate scenario of a non-supportive close relationship does occur, the risk is for this relationship to become toxic and harmful. Ultimately, you lose yourself because you cannot grow or are not being allowed to grow. The only solution for this, I can see, is professional help.

The motivator's curse is: Whether you like it or not, your success, or even partial success, to make something better of yourself is motivational to others. But you might unintentionally push away, threaten or shame those in your support group who cannot see past or deal with their hurt. This hurt might cause these "support people" to try and hinder your growth so they can pull you back down to their level again.

Most people who reach out to me for support are initially scared of opinions and judgments. But it is not the unkind words from close friends and family that they fear. In my case, I spent my entire life feeling trapped in the opinions and judgements of the people in my immediate family.

The Cop-out

My Weigh-Less group leader invited me to present my first open meeting talk the December after rejoining Weigh-Less. Weigh-Less group meetings are ordinarily private and only for members. Open meetings are those which are open to the public. They are usually fun as the group leader advertises the meeting, organises snacks, and arranges a guest speaker. It is an honour to be invited to be the guest speaker for such a talk.

During the almost three years it took me to get to goal weight, my group leader frequently invited me as a guest speaker, not just to the group I attended. After reaching goal weight, I wanted to talk at more open group meetings across Johannesburg. My group leader was fully supportive of this and tried to make it happen.

I was making good progress on my goal of reaching more people through open meeting talks until lockdown happened, and we were all stuck at home. On the first Tuesday of the lockdown, I was supposed to be the guest speaker at an open meeting talk for the group I attended. That presentation would have been my first post-goal-weight talk for this group, and I was very excited about it. It is always special for me to talk to the group which was "home" to my weight loss journey.

I had my talk prepared and felt rather down about not presenting it anymore. I could not simply sit and do nothing while watching my opportunities being taken away from me — I had a huge desire to share my story.

Not knowing anything about the new domain I was bound to find myself in, I thought that perhaps I should do my talk online. The only way I knew how was to do the presentation on Facebook. I just happened to know about Facebook live videos because my Pilates coach did live videos now and again.

Mart-Mari, you are a software engineer, for crying out loud! How difficult can this video thing be to figure out?

Much more difficult than I thought! I didn't have a Facebook page at that stage, only my personal Facebook profile. I managed to schedule my live talk and even advertise it on our Weigh-Less group. I also promoted it to the neighbourhood groups to which I belong. People must have thought that I was crazy, and I probably was. Crazy I may have been, but I was determined not to let the lockdown get in the way of my 2020 goals. I was more out of my depth and comfort zone than ever before.

I have since realised that one's growth zone can not be found where one's comfort zone is.

On the Saturday afternoon of my first live video, I got to my desk early. I have a desktop computer without a built-in webcam or microphone, but I had a small basic separate webcam that we bought a few years ago to chat to my in-laws and a headset that I use for online meetings at work. I still use that webcam for my online talks but have since made another plan for the microphone. Conscientiously I started my live video feed a few minutes before the advertised time of 15:00 — first mistake ...

I wanted to be prepared but have since realised that people don't appreciate waiting for a talk to start. And I didn't prepare something to talk about before my planned main video content either. Nothing pushes up your stress levels more than seeing people joining and knowing that they could see you sitting there with nothing to say. Perhaps I should have babbled on, as that would have prevented my second mistake ...

On starting the live video, I received a Facebook notification that my live video has started. I clicked on that notification, thinking that that was what I was supposed to do. However, that link opened my live video stream, which meant I was then tuned in to watch the video of myself as a viewer simultaneously as when I was presenting it. I didn't realise this as I was still sitting there waiting for people to join. It was only at 15:00 when I started talking that I, and everyone else who had tuned in, heard the echo.

I had no idea how to fix this echo. It was only afterwards that I realised the echo was because I simultaneously tuned in to my talk as a viewer — a profound 'face palm' moment. I tried taking my headphones down at one stage to talk directly into the headphones' microphone. That solved the echo problem for me but made it worst for everyone else. Via the live comments, someone suggested that I turn off my headphones' speaker under my system's settings. Only once I turned that off we could continue without the echo. We were already almost ten minutes into the talk, and I was beyond flustered. Nevertheless, I persevered and managed to complete the speech presentation that I'd prepared.

I felt so embarrassed by this mistake. Every time I shared that first video, I warned people to skip through the first part. Only about six months later, after I started my own Facebook page, did I figure out how to download and edit out the first part of my first video. The edited video is now on my Facebook page, but the original one is still on my personal Facebook profile. It will forever be special to me. It turned out to be the start of something I enjoy doing.

Despite my mistakes and embarrassment, people seemed to love that first video, and I received the most incredible feedback and support. The community's support meant so much that I decided to do another live video the following Saturday. By the end of our hard lockdown, I did an entire series of four live videos. I presented the last video of that series three weeks before starting my sessions with Therapist.

Almost five months into my sessions with Therapist, I had a powerful message pressing on my heart and made me feel inspired to do another live presentation. This message was about emotional eating. During the last live video of my lockdown series, I burst into tears towards the end while talking about my fear of regaining. After my emotional display, I felt convinced that I would never do another live video ever again. But it seemed like I could not stay away from the water. Here I was contemplating another live video, and when the inspiration hits, I believe one has to act on it.

My emotional eating video went incredibly well, with almost no mistakes, and to date, it is still the best-received and most-watched video out of all my videos. It was also the first live video presented on my Facebook page. I am very proud of it.

During the therapy session following my emotional eating video, I shared the video and how proud I felt about it with Therapist. He responded to my enthusiasm with a fascinating exercise for me to do using this video. All of my therapy challenges were usually interesting. Still, sometimes, one like this pops up that leaves me surprised at Therapist's creativity and ability to think on his feet. I threw a lot of weird stuff at him in a session — the poor man.

Therapist asked me if I could try watching my emotional eating video as if I was my mum, in other words, through her eyes. And then jot down what I think her response to the video would have been.

I felt incredibly proud of my emotional eating video; presenting an online video like that was something I never thought I would be able to do. I thought everything about this video was perfect. However, when I tried to watch the video through my mum's eyes, I just got criticism. I saw everything that I had done wrong. I saw only mistakes. I felt stupid and that my message was dull and pointless and not worth sharing. It made me so angry. I was furious! I felt proud of my video, but critique was all I could think of when trying to imagine my mum's reaction. Other people, strangers, had had such positive responses to it. I also believed that the message meant something to others. Yet my mum's imagined reaction made me feel as if I should be ashamed about the video and delete it. I never even considered deleting my first video; that did cause me embarrassment!

Was this what Therapist wanted me to see?

Was the imagined response from my mum some form of inner voice that I carried with me? If so, then I had probably been burdening myself with it for years. Did I still listen to it? How much? A lot? A little? I had so many questions.

At my next session, I shared the feedback from this debriefing exercise with Therapist. He responded that although my perception of her being critical of my video was probably correct, it was not a typical mother's response. I should try to imagine what her real proud response would have been.

Puzzled, I looked at Therapist and asked, "I don't understand. Do you expect me to start making up responses on her behalf now?"

Almost immediately, he replied, "No, no, no ... You are too analytical again."

Apparently, I was analytical — who knew?

Therapist explained: "What would your response or reaction have been if it was your sister who did the video?"

Without hesitation, I answered, "I would've been so proud of her. If she could manage to lose eighty kilograms, work on herself and have the confidence to do a live online video, I would have been the proudest sister in the entire world. I don't think there would've been a person that I would've not shared her success with."

"And if it was one of your children who did the video?" Therapist asked.

"I would also be proud. How can a mum not be proud when her child does something like that?" I answered.

"What do you think your sister would say in response to your video?" Therapist continued asking.

"Firstly, she probably would not even have watched it. But if she did, she would have hated it and shut me out of her life even more. She would have been jealous and vindictive."

Somehow I could understand that being a mum or a sister meant that you were automatically proud of your children and sister. Yet when asked what my mum and sister's reactions would be, I would always list the negative ones.

"Can you see that your mum and sister's reactions are not normal?"

After my sister's diagnosis of Manic Depression, I could see my mum's behaviour reflected at me through my sister's behaviour. And even more so in the last few months of her life when she was not taking her medication. I have a strong suspicion that my mum probably also suffered from some form of depression. Still, no doctor ever diagnosed her as depressed, and it was undoubtedly never treated.

Therapist explained, "An untreated manic depressed person's self-esteem is already very low. The only way they see themselves feeling better about themselves is to try to pull those around them down to their level. They are never going to be supportive or uplifting. Not as long as they remain untreated."

My mum and sister's behaviours towards me were not how a typical mum and sister would behave. For my sanity, I needed to imagine what their natural responses should have been, or at the very least understand that the internal voices I hear from them were not the real them. It was my interaction with their illnesses.

Usually, in the evening following a session, I would sit and discuss my therapy with my husband. That evening when I tried to explain my session to my husband, his response was, "But that is like giving them a 'Get out of jail free'-card."

I guess it is. It is a cop-out for my mum and my sister. But somehow, I feel that this explanation has brought me a tremendous amount of peace.

Running

I step out onto the tarmac. My sandalled feet do not know the feel of the road. I decided to walk downhill. My skirt offers resistance to the wind. Walking in a skirt with sandals must look so weird to people passing by, I think. No, maybe not. It probably looks like I am just walking to visit one of my neighbours. I take a right turn at the bottom of our street. Am I supposed to walk with or against the traffic? Against the traffic, surely, that would make more sense. That way, I can see a car approaching. My right turn leads me to my first uphill. Walking is not as easy as I thought it would be. Not with sandals. I need to rethink my choice of footwear. What route would be a suitable road to walk? I should walk the same way that I drive; at least I won't get lost then. The road looks different on foot from in a car, funny how that is. Is that always the case? What do people think of while walking? Or do they look around them, taking in their surroundings? I see someone else jogging. I raise my hand to greet her, and she nods back politely. She is wearing earphones. I need to get some of those. But people visiting their neighbours don't wear earphones. Perhaps I can fake being on a call? That might not be safe. Let's rather leave the earphones for now. I take a left turn. This road is busy. I'm not too fond of it. I need to find another way. I take the next right turn. I've been walking for fifteen minutes, time to turn around. I start walking back the same way that I came. My feet are hurting where the shoe straps dig into my skin. Wearing sandals was not a good idea. But I cannot wear sneakers with a skirt, that will look suspicious. I finally arrived back at our front gate. Home sweet home. This mission was challenging, but I was successful. I have just completed my first thirty-minute walk. I wonder if anyone noticed that I didn't leave my house to visit a neighbour?

— *Me on my first attempt at walking*

*   *   *

One of my favourite things to say when asked about exercising is, "You can never outrun a bad diet!"

People are quick to assume that they must start exercising when dieting. As if exercising would give them "credits" and allow them to cheat on their eating plan. Neither of the above is true.

The first time I did Weigh-Less, I exercised. I went to the gym, mainly for cardio, and I did Pilates there as well. I loved Pilates, I still do, but I was never a runner. That first time around on Weigh-Less, I lost well and at a good pace, but I was seven years younger and only had one child then.

When I rejoined Weigh-Less to start my weight loss mission of eighty kilograms, I did not intend to exercise. I was too big *and heavy*. It would have been far too uncomfortable. I don't think I would have been able to find exercise clothes to suit my frame. I struggled to find suitably sized dresses and only had one dress left in the closet that still fitted me, definitely no pants and for sure no sneakers.

My husband was sceptical of my plan not to exercise. He believed that I did well the first time at Weigh-Less because of the exercise. Because the Weigh-Less eating plan is a lot of food, my husband felt that I would gain weight if I did not exercise. This disagreement around exercise was the only area where my husband didn't support my dieting plans completely. He was on board with everything else.

Despite my husband's feelings around exercise, I started Weigh-Less in February 2017, and, as the weeks progressed, I lost consistently week after week — without exercising! By December 2017, I had still not done any exercise but had lost about thirty-five kilograms. My husband's Christmas present to me that year was a Garmin fitness watch that could measure my heart rate. A subtle hint?

At that stage, I was still more than forty kilos overweight and leading a completely sedentary lifestyle. I was incredibly unfit, but I thought I was doing rather well, even without exercising. But I realised that my husband was right and that I would have to start sooner or later. I was not keen on taking my new watch and hitting the gym. I wanted something where I could chicken out if I saw that it was not working for me! A gym had enrolment fees and a contract, and I had experienced the gym scene before; I was not keen on displaying my excess more than forty kilograms in that scene just yet.

I thought the most straightforward thing to do would be to start walking. Walking did not require me to join anything, and I didn't even need to drive anywhere. My medical aid had a rewards program whereby you earned points when exercising for thirty minutes or more at a heart rate above 70%. I wanted to give that a go.

A few days after Christmas, I started walking. My goal was to keep my heart rate between 70% and 80% of the maximum heart rate for my age for at least thirty minutes. My plan was as follows: when I saw that my heart rate was too low, I would walk a bit faster, and if it were too high, I would walk a little slower. My heart rate would go relatively high in the beginning despite me walking a reasonable flat route. I was too unfit. But I tried sticking it out for the thirty minutes required by my rewards program.

This walking continued for almost the whole of 2018. As I became fitter, I started to find it challenging to keep my heart rate in the correct zone. I adapted my route to include more inclines. It certainly helped that our neighbourhood is very hilly. I even had to extend my course at one stage because I started walking faster and didn't want to stop till my thirty minutes were over. I was gradually improving!

The hernia operation I had in April 2018 did put a damper on my walking. I walked as much as I could up to the day before my procedure and then spent just more than a week in hospital with the physiotherapist encouraging me to stroll for short distances. I continued doing this when I got home but outside in the fresh air. The unevenness of the tarmac was a challenge, but before I knew it, I was back to walking the same route and at the same pace as before my operation.

My sister committed suicide in November 2018, and I spent a great deal of December 2018 selling baby goods. I felt overwhelmed, and walking was one of the few things that kept me sane. One day that December, I discovered that it had become impossible to keep my heart rate in the desired zone when walking downhill, no matter how fast I walked. While I was walking and becoming frustrated by my heart rate not increasing despite my best effort, I decided that the only option is to jog the downhills. I started running right then and there.

I continued jogging the downhills and walking the uphills until I noticed I had the same problem walking uphill. So I started jogging those out too! Jogging out the uphills was a bit more challenging as I couldn't manage to jog up a hill from the bottom to the top without taking a break. So I set myself goals, like jogging up to a specific tree and then the next week to a particular house and so on, until one day I could jog continuously up to the top.

The route that I jogged back then was a three-kilometre route, and initially, it took me just more than thirty minutes to run that distance. My course taking just more than thirty minutes to complete, was great, as I was still sticking to my medical rewards program's exercise requirement. It started taking less than thirty minutes to complete that route after a while, and I needed to regroup. So I worked out a five-kilometre course, and later, when that became too easy, I worked towards running my original five-kilometre route twice over weekends to make it ten kilometres in all. I still run the shorter five-kilometre course on weekdays and aim to do at least forty kilometres per week, more if I can and have the time.

Today I feel incredibly proud to call myself a runner and am lost for words to express just how much I love running. I never thought it was something that I, who was at one stage just over eighty kilograms overweight, would be able to do, never mind enjoy. I have fallen in love with running, head over heels.

Just before lockdown started, on Valentines day 2020, I took part in my first ten-kilometres race; it was also the first time I ran further than five kilometres. I joined one of the buses during the race, and we had a great bus "driver" coaching us through the entire race. When I crossed the finishing line, I teared up. At that moment, the sheer enormity of what I, who at one stage could not even bend down to tie my shoelaces, had achieved was too much.

Over lockdown levels five and four, in March and April 2020, I ran three-hundred-and-sixty-eight kilometres on a short, forty-meter garden route around a tree in my front yard. By the end of 2020, I ran a half-marathon to celebrate the first anniversary of reaching my goal weight. My goal is to keep improving my pace and extending my running distance and endurance.

Exercising did ultimately cause me to lose weight slower. It took me about eleven months to lose the first half of my eighty kilograms without exercising and just under two years to lose the remaining half while exercising.

However, starting to exercise was worth it, as running has done so much for me. If it weren't for running, I would've never loosened the dust needed to bring my relationship with my mother to Therapist's attention, and if I hadn't done that, we might never have started our therapy sessions. When Therapist ended our sessions, running became my therapy.

When I run, I release more than just sweat. Nothing and no one bothers me when I run. I turn on my music, but I turn off the world. My feet hit the tarmac, and I enter a zone of meditation, navigating the road on autopilot. Sometimes, a few minutes into a run, I don't even hear my music anymore. At that stage, it is just me and my thoughts. Often I will cry while running, especially when I am busy "writing". I have written this entire book while running. I think about what I want to write while out on the road; then I jot down a few ideas when I get home and flesh out those ideas in the afternoons or the evenings after supper. This book came about by more than four hundred kilometres on the tarmac. I am convinced that if it weren't for running, I would never have been able to write.

Running also helped me tone my body. I am proud of my six-pack. I am also incredibly proud of how I look after losing eighty kilograms. I do have some excess skin, but not sufficient to complain about. I manage my excess skin by dry-brushing, running and my Pilates classes. I can see how my body and skin has improved over time, and I look forward to seeing how it will continue improving.

Overall, my husband was not correct about me not losing weight if I didn't exercise. I would have been able to lose all eighty kilograms without ever exercising. But exercising gave me so much more than just weight benefits. My fitness watch was the best Christmas present ever!

The Fruit Of Being Myself

Something I am often asked, usually by overweight people, is, 'What is it like to be thin? Is it everything you hoped it would be?'

These questions make me think of the Old Testament and the promised land in the Bible. What will it be like in the promised land? Will we finally be happy there?

Therapist once said that following a journey was like taking a hike up a mountain. As my tour guide, he could explain the view from the top to me, but I would only know what it is genuinely like once I have seen it myself. He was, of course, not talking about my weight loss journey as I've already lost my weight before I started working with him.

From a technical point of view, I created this book by creating empty files on my computer for all the individual chapters and then arranging these files in the order I believed made sense. This high-level plan worked well for me as I liked adding little 'thought snippets' to the individual files as I contemplated them. I often deviated from my original high-level plan as I renamed, scrapped, and reordered many chapters. Some chapters were too long and gave birth to two or three more chapters.

Writing this book was an agile project, and I felt comfortable working that way as that is what I am used to as a professional software engineer. Originally I named this chapter 'The Fruit of Being Thin'. The idea was to answer what it is like to be thin. Initially, this chapter was right at the end of the book. I thought it would be a nod to a fairy tale ending — and she lived happily ever after, thin.

I used to believe that being thin was the answer to all my problems. Everything would be better if I could lose the extra weight I carried.

Everyone would like me then; I would be respected for my intellect and not overlooked. I would be worthy of love. Clothes would no longer be a problem as I could shop at more shops with a greater variety of options. I would also not be constantly tired anymore. And I will have a better body image while enjoying a more fulfilling and adventurous sex life.

As I started writing this chapter — while out on the road running — I realised that the advantages of weighing a "normal" weight had very little to do with the weight itself. Since starting to post about my weight loss on social media, I have had other overweight people reach out to me to meet me in person. I usually meet these people for a coffee date, and the first question I typically ask them is to explain why they would like to lose weight. The top three reasons are:

I want to be happy.

I want to be healthier.

I want to look better.

I want to look at each of these reasons individually. If these are the top reasons people want to lose weight, then it makes sense that people would expect me to answer, "I am happier, healthier and better looking since reaching my goal weight."

While that might be true, 'Happier, healthier and better looking' are not just the fruit of my weight loss. They are the fruit of me finally honestly being myself!

I want to lose weight to be happy.

The one thing I can say now, after losing eighty kilograms, is that losing weight will not make you happy. If you were miserable before losing weight, likely, you would still be dissatisfied after losing weight. You can even be troubled while being a normal weight.

When somebody tells me they want to lose weight to be happy, I always ask them if they currently know someone who is overweight but happy. Every single person I have asked that question to thus far does know of another person who is both heavy and happy at the same time. Happiness is an internal state of mind. You can choose to be happy, which usually has a lot to do with being thankful and appreciative of what you already have.

However, I am happier thin than I was when I was fat. But it was not a case of me suddenly acquiring this state of happiness when I reached my goal weight. My joy came from an inner peace that I only experienced after freeing myself from years — a lifetime — of shame that I carried with me. I disassociated from shame by bringing to the light everything that has happened to me or that I felt ashamed of. In many cases, I made myself aware of the issues I've carried with me for the first time. As I became aware of my problems, I made myself extraordinarily vulnerable and decided to share what I have been through with other people — even strangers.

I've experienced, like Brené Brown had said, that shame genuinely multiplies in isolation but starts to disappear when shared. When everybody knows what you have done or been through, there is nothing to hide or lie about anymore.

Sharing my journey has also brought me happiness as it gave a new purpose to my life. I could help and inspire others through my story. Being able to do that is something that makes me insanely happy. I also discovered that I enjoy writing and presenting. Both writing and presenting are skills that I would like to continue working on and improve. I believe this is my destiny, but I never had the confidence to embrace it.

My marriage has never been happier than it is now as well. My husband and I communicate incredibly well. He treats me like a queen; I feel desirable when I am with him. My sex life has dramatically improved, not just because of losing weight but also because I am more confident. I never say no to my husband. In fact, I am the one initiating sex confidently now. There is no begging for sex in our marriage. The only pleading that happens is in our bedroom when I request my husband to stop — a woman can only handle so many orgasms in one session!

I want to lose weight to be healthier.

Losing weight to be healthier is possibly the weight loss reason that makes the most sense — to me, at least. When I get someone who lists being healthier as one reason to lose weight, I encourage this person to expand on what being "healthy" means, be more specific and make the goal measurable. For example, if the person wants to be fitter, what does that imply? Do they want to be able to run a five-kilometre route? How fast do they wish to run those five kilos? Being able to measure progress and see results are great motivators during a weight loss journey. Besides fitness — blood pressure, blood sugar, and cholesterol are all health measures that can significantly improve with weight loss. I have seen many people in our Weigh-Less group stop their blood pressure and cholesterol medicine, even recovering from or needing less treatment for type two diabetes.

While still obese, I had issues with high blood pressure. My blood pressure has dropped significantly, and I have since discovered I have low blood pressure. However, my most significant health improvement had been having the hernia operation that I needed. Hopefully, my children will never have to grow up with memories of me being sick in bed and struggling with hernia-trapped intestines.

Becoming a runner has also greatly improved my fitness. My average resting heart rate is forty beats per minute. I am no fitness expert, but the people I've told this to before said that my resting heart rate is excellent and an indication of being fit. I enjoy pushing my body and trying new things. For the first time in my life, I can do that — and it feels incredible!

I want to lose weight to look better.

I am not a fan of losing weight to look better. I believe a person should feel good about the way they look even when they are overweight. When I meet with someone that feels very strongly about looking better as a reason for losing weight, I encourage them to make this goal measurable. 'Looking better' cannot be a goal as it is so subject to opinion. Will you believe you are looking better when others start telling you that you do, or when you think that yourself when looking in the mirror? If I were to wait until I felt I looked better, I might still be dieting. And if I were to wait till other people complimented me, then I would've quitted prematurely.

I never had 'looking better' as a weight loss goal, although I did have an associated fashion goal. About five months into my weight loss journey, I bought a skirt. A friend, who happens to be a personal stylist, was having a second-hand clothing sale. Because I decided at the start of my weight loss journey to not keep clothes — apart from two dresses for my open meeting talks — as they became too big, I had second-hand oversized garments that I could donate to her sale. My friend gave me some vouchers to spend at her event to thank me for my donation.

Among the sale items was a beautiful black skirt. It was dramatic and romantic, and I immediately fell in love with it. The only problem was that it was a size ten. I was still a size twenty-four then, but the pickings at the sale in my size were very slim. I loved this skirt so much that I decided to buy it even though it was far too small for me. My friend eyed me very sceptically. I kept this skirt in my closet for my entire weight loss journey. Now and again, I would try it on to see if it fitted yet, but it wasn't till the end of 2019 that it did. What a joyous day that was! The skirt is still a favourite.

The story of my dramatic black skirt is the ultimate of non-scale goals, in my opinion, and when I have someone who wants to use 'looking better' as a goal, I try to get them to follow a similar approach to making their goal measurable.

My stylist friend started a Whatsapp based styling program in January 2020 called #styleBuddy. I eagerly joined her program as I wanted to learn how to dress correctly for my new body shape. Her program has meant and continues to mean a lot to me, and slowly but surely, I am learning how to dress. I cannot even explain the joy it brings me to go shopping for clothes now. I can take an armful of items into the dressing room with me, and most of the time, they all fit. For the first time in my life, I have options for clothes, and I don't have to settle for whatever is available in the largest size the store stocks. And I love the days when I wear my black skirt; it is always a special reminder to me of how far I've come.

I found working on a positive body image to be extremely difficult. I can honestly say that I still didn't think of myself as looking better for months, almost a year, after reaching goal weight. Years of teasing and negative comments broke my body image beyond repair — I thought I was ugly. Anybody, even my husband, could tell me that I was beautiful, but it would not matter. I especially didn't believe my husband as I thought he was obliged to call me beautiful. Looking better was the most challenging fruit for me to see.

Therapist had me work through just about all of his body image courses and exercises, but nothing helped! When I looked in the mirror, I would still find a way to see something I didn't like — and then it was all I saw.

The turning point came through my boudoir shoot. I have a wonderful photographer friend who has been taking photos of my children from their baby days. We have also been going to her for family photos yearly since a year into my weight loss journey. In 2020, we couldn't make our family shoot because of the lockdown, so the two of us started discussing a boudoir shoot for later in 2020. I wanted the boudoir shoot to celebrate the eighty kilograms that I lost.

The boudoir shoot included professional makeup, even false eyelashes, and as I hardly ever wear makeup, I already felt spoiled. My photographer friend directed me so well for the shoot, getting all my best angles and hiding all my flaws. I was so nervous, at one stage the makeup and my wedding ring were the only things I was wearing!

My boudoir shoot was an incredibly liberating experience, and I have never felt sexier. The photos also turned out fantastically. There is something about seeing yourself in print looking like a hot supermodel; it only makes you feel good about yourself. I have since had some of those photos framed for our bedroom, and it is a daily reminder that I have done something extraordinary and looking like that is one of the fruit I get to reap.

However, the most significant fruit that I reaped from losing weight was increased self-confidence. I genuinely believe now there is nothing that I cannot do. I was so determined when lockdown started not to let my 2020 goals drift away from me that I began to present online. And, of course, I started writing, which ended up with me writing this book. If you had told me even a week before reaching goal weight that those were things I would do, I would not have believed you. Even after getting to goal weight, I would have been sceptical.

It is not just the physical difference in my body that has increased my confidence. I had a massive mountain to climb that felt insurmountable initially, but somehow I managed to do it. And if I can lose eighty kilograms, there must be very little else that I cannot do.

I wanted to end this chapter by illustrating what it is like watching my son now when he swims at a gala. But because of Covid, parents have not been allowed to spectate any live sporting events yet. But one day, I believe I will have that opportunity again, and I will blog about it. Look out for that blog post!

My Sex Testimony

His hands make me want to follow his every move as he unrolls and smooths out the satin restraint. He pins my forearms down with his and then masterfully ties my wrists together above my head. Before picking up and securing a soft blindfold over my eyes, he gives me a long and lingering kiss.

I love being at his mercy, wondering where he will touch me next or what his next move will be. Being in our bed with him is the one place where I don't mind not being in control. I am his. I am his wife. I trust him completely, and he can do whatever it is that he wants to do. Together we had built a life that we love. Being with him and us enjoying each other is a big, essential and beautiful part of this life that we love.

His tongue circles one of my nipples while he plays with the other nipple, gently rolling it between his thumb and forefinger. He sucks and tucks and at times gently bites down, protruding and erecting each nipple — giving them all the attention that they deserve.

He runs his tongue down the side of my neck from just below my ear, stopping to plant a kiss now and then softly. He goes about it agonisingly slow, making my toes curl and the hair on my forearms and the back of my neck rise. Then he stops again for a long, deep and intimate kiss.

He moves down my body with his mouth until he reaches the apex of my thighs — his favourite place to be. I am his favourite place to be. He knows my body so well. He knows exactly which buttons to press and how.

He deeply inhales and starts paying attention to my clitoris with his mouth. He follows short and quick flicks with the tip of his tongue by extended and slow movements all along the length of my vulva — only stopping to blow soft kisses or tease with his fingers inside. He repeats and continues to do so until I find my release, and he can savour the fruit of it.

Having just tasted me, he extends himself forward to meet me at face level again, his mouth finding mine. His tongue circles and explores the inside of my mouth, sharing the sweet fruit, before he heads back down for another course.

* * *

In February 2020, I sent a friend of mine a message to wish her a very happy birthday. This friend of mine s born in the same year as me and thus just a few months older.

She messaged me back, "Thank you! We are getting old now."

"Speak for yourself. I feel like I am getting younger," I jested back.

"You will have to share your secret with me," she said.

I thought I might as well tell her what I believe to be the truth. She had been a good friend of mine for many years. We didn't see each other that often in person, though, so I had enough time to work off my embarrassment before I would see her face to face again. I replied, "The secret is lots of mind-blowing, amazing and squirting orgasms!"

For most of my sexually active life, I believed that the female orgasm was a myth. I heard no evidence of it in casual conversations with other women; I didn't know of anyone that had ever experienced it. I thought those who were writing about it on the internet were lying for sensation purposes. On the other hand, my husband never stopped believing that female orgasms were real and that I would have an orgasm one day in some way — no scepticism on my part could convince him otherwise.

At the beginning of our sexually active lives, sex was boring and monotonous. My husband, who was still my boyfriend at that stage, and I were both very overweight. Not that our being overweight ever stopped us, but we didn't experiment much. Just the excitement of being with each other and not knowing what we were doing and figuring it out as we went along was enough. Our initial contraceptives were condoms. The most experimentation we did was in using different types of textured condoms.

I lacked any confidence then as well. I wouldn't even dare buy condoms myself. I didn't feel sexy, confident or desirable in the bedroom. For my entire life up to that point, getting naked and dressing happened by myself in private. Undressing and looking at myself in the mirror was already not an activity that I enjoyed. To suddenly be naked with someone else and allow this other person to be inside of you as well. It was a scary thought, and I didn't feel entirely comfortable letting someone else see me that way. But I also wanted to have sex and experience it — hormones are silly! I tried to hide as much as possible during sex, not allowing my boyfriend to explore too much. If I could have used a sheet with a hole cut out and placed that over me during sex, I swear I would've.

The thing I enjoyed most about sex in those early years was the silly games that we'd use to play beforehand. My husband is hilariously funny and has always been so. We'd used to tease each other, getting rid of more clothes as we went along. These games helped me relax and set the mood as light and playful as possible. But once we'd reached the point where it was time for penetration, it was always the same: missionary position until male ejaculation, and that was the end of it. I didn't fancy sex. I liked the play beforehand, but that was the only thing I enjoyed about sex. Sex itself wasn't something that particularly rocked my boat. My husband, still boyfriend then, enjoyed it, and because I wanted to make him happy, it became essential to me to at least make an effort.

One day, after a scare with a condom that tore, we had to go to the pharmacy to purchase a morning-after pill. We were still unmarried then. My parents didn't know what we were up to, and a surprise pregnancy was not my idea of breaking the news either.

"Okay, so you just explain the situation to the pharmacist and ask if there is anything you can take to prevent becoming pregnant," my boyfriend asked when we stopped in front of the pharmacy.

I replied: "So you mean I have to tell the pharmacist, a stranger, that

I had sex and the condom that my boyfriend bought broke?"

"You don't have to tell him that I bought the condom."

"What!? No, no. I don't want to tell a stranger that I had sex!"

"Would you rather tell your mother that you are pregnant? You have to explain the situation to get the right medication."

"I am most probably not pregnant."

"But what if you are?"

"Can you not do it?"

"No, I already bought the condoms. Certainly, you can do this?"

"But it was one of the condoms that you bought that broke."

"For crying out loud! It was not my fault. But alright, I'll do the talking then. Come, let's go."

"No, I am not going to come with you."

"So not only do you not want to do the talking, you don't even want to go into the pharmacy?"

"Yes, I want to stay in the car. I will turn all shades of red if I stand next to you while you explain our dilemma. I'll wait for you."

"And you don't think this is embarrassing for me also? Will you at least take the medication if there is something you can use? What if they ask specific questions that only you can answer?"

"Yes, I would take the medication; I don't want to be pregnant either. And if there are any questions you can return to the car to ask me. Besides, is it not cool for men to be sexually active? You are responsible, right; I am sure the pharmacist will see it like that."

On his return, once back in the car, my boyfriend shared his dismay: "The pharmacist was a woman! I have never had a more uncomfortable conversation in my life. We need to make another plan for this not to happen again."

"Yes, we can not have sex."

"Or you can start birth control."

I was already twenty-one years old by then. I didn't need my mother's permission to start contraceptives. The doctor I went to was charming and concerned about me requiring contraceptives. He still tried to convince me to talk to my mum first — which, of course, I didn't do. However, oral contraceptives placed a massive damper on my libido.

Sex was already not fun for me. Contraceptives made me feel like I did not even want to make an effort for my boyfriend's pleasure either. Sex became a chore and something I thought I was obliged to do.

My boyfriend wasn't happy with the situation. He didn't want to have sex with me if he had to beg me each time for it. He started insisting even more that we focus all our efforts on getting me to orgasm. I felt that his reasons for being so keen to try were selfish. I thought he believed that if I would enjoy sex more, he would also be getting more sex. I didn't want him to try to get me to orgasm. I didn't even want sex in the first place! His suggestion that he played with me until I orgasm didn't sound like a good suggestion.

Consequently, when I did agree to him trying to do that, I couldn't let myself go. I became annoyed when nothing happened, which put me off trying even more. Ultimately I ended up always denying him whenever he wanted to try.

After getting married, when we decided that we wanted to start a family, I stopped my oral contraceptives. I could, within a few days, feel some form of libido returning. Although I felt like a different person when I was not taking my contraceptive medication, my medication served another purpose. My medication regulated my monthly cycle and made my menstruation bleeding less.

I had been struggling with iron deficiency anemia from about eighteen years old. Doctor after doctor blamed my heavy menstrual bleeding as the cause of my iron deficiency. But there was not much we could do about my heavy menstrual bleeding then. I still wanted children, and most of the solutions on offer required me not to desire to have any more children. The doctor who prescribed me contraceptives initially said that the contraceptives would help regulate my heavy menstrual bleeding as well, which they did. When I stopped taking them, along with some of my libido, my heavy menstrual bleeding also returned. Fortunately, I fell pregnant very quickly. Along with breastfeeding and being pregnant five times and giving birth four times, I managed to avoid periods almost entirely for the better part of nine years.

Before my last pregnancy, I had the Mirena inserted. We weren't sure if we wanted to have another child, but I didn't want to start oral contraceptives again. I thought the Mirena would be a good solution for me, but I was wrong. It was a costly disaster! I continually bled for almost six months with the Mirena fitted and felt very down and depressed. The hormonal cocktail of the Mirena did not work for me. I opted to have it removed. On the day that I had it removed, I could already feel how my mood lifted. Within a month after removing it, I was pregnant again! My husband had always said that I was like an old car: I started with the first push.

During my last pregnancy, my husband went for a vasectomy. We were sure then that we did not want any more children. My husband said that he would take one for the team. I was delighted. If he were to go for a vasectomy, I would not need to use contraceptives again.

When our youngest started weaning, my husband decided that it is time that we again focus our sexual efforts on me achieving an orgasm. He bought us our first vibrator, convinced that this was the thing that was going to get the job done.

We tried, we read up, and then we tried again. We could not get the most effective usage of it figured out. My husband was doing most of the research, though — perhaps that was the problem? Maybe the one with the vulva should've been the one researching, but I was not as invested as he was in getting results from this toy.

The strange thing about sex and sex toys is that nobody talks about them. There is no safe place where one can ask for advice without being ridiculed. I didn't know Therapist then; otherwise, I would've asked him, seeing that he is a sex therapist. Our sex toy did not bring us any joy — or we were just too dumb to use it correctly. At one stage, my husband even went so far as to deny himself pleasure, i.e. penetration, if I didn't get satisfaction, i.e. an orgasm, first. That just placed unnecessary pressure on me. All the vibrator did was cause a sensation of pins and needles that was just uncomfortable.

Eventually, one evening, after following some advice my husband discovered online about clitoral and g-spot stimulation and alternating between them to avoid the pins and needles feeling and also about using additional lubrication, I managed to reach my first orgasm! Both of us were stunned. By then, I considered female orgasms a myth, and I was just about ready to give up on my husband's mission.

When I finally experienced that first orgasm, I felt like I wanted to shout it out from the rooftops. I do not have the vocabulary to describe what an orgasm feels like justly. There is very little else that can compare to that feeling. The following morning, my husband described it as this massive thing that we have achieved but could not share with anyone else. He felt like he wanted to phone someone and tell them — as if it was something newsworthy. I would've died if he did that!

My first orgasm, unfortunately, didn't cause subsequent orgasms to come effortlessly. It was a few months before I had another one. My very heavy menstrual bleeding also returned in the meanwhile, and its return hampered our efforts even more. I would bleed every twenty-one days for at least seven days, losing as much as one hundred millilitres of blood per day on my heaviest bleeding days. I could measure this because I used a menstrual cup. It wasn't long before my iron was at an all-time low.

Along with my low iron came excuses of being too tired for sex. I also had four small children. I was morbidly obese. I did not feel good about myself or the way that I looked. I couldn't even use contraceptives as an excuse anymore as I wasn't taking them at that stage. I had managed to reach orgasms, which was terrific, but even that couldn't convince me to have more sex. I started running out of excuses, so I found new ones, while the truth was: I started feeling entitled to refuse sex.

Me having success on my weight loss journey did improve things in the bedroom — slowly but surely. But there were still too many other issues bothering me. In January 2019, my doctor recommended that I start oral contraceptives yet again to see if we could regulate my menstrual cycle. I didn't want to begin contraceptives again. I hated what contraceptives did to me. But I also hated feeling so dead tired all the time. I agreed to her recommendation, but by August 2019, I decided to quit them. I couldn't deal with the side effects. In the last year of my weight loss journey, I wanted to already be at my goal weight by my birthday in May 2019, but the stupid contraceptives made it so difficult for me to lose weight. My libido was also wholly non-existent. I hated how the contraceptives made me feel. I hated the person I was when I took them.

A friend invited me to join them for their church's women's camp weekend in August 2019. One of the presentations that weekend was from their pastor's wife. Her presentation was about the importance and beauty of sex in marriage. It was an outstanding presentation and made me realise that what I was doing in refusing sex so often was not correct. Even if I was tired, had four kids, and my libido was not what it should be — none of those was valid excuses. I decided then that I would make sex a priority and not refuse my husband anymore.

That decision turned out to be one of the best decisions that I had ever made. I prioritised and made time for sex — my husband was just happy to oblige. Sex became such an essential part of our marriage to the point of being sexually active on each non-period day. My orgasms started increasing in frequency and intensity. However, we were still using the missionary position most of the time — not the most exciting or most interesting.

To prevent boredom, we agreed to start experimenting more. My husband's initial goal of getting me to orgasm, although it took us many years to get there, was a good idea. We added another goal which was for me to ejaculate (squirt). Me finally reaching my goal weight, dressing better, and growing in confidence improved our sex lives significantly. I started wearing sexier outfits and lingerie in our bedroom and was less hesitant for my husband to explore more of my body very intimately. We started trying different positions and introduced more sex toys.

By the time we started participating in Therapist's courses, I had thought we were doing pretty well. I'd managed to reach orgasms reliably by then and had even figured out how to squirt — our second sex goal. At that stage, I couldn't even remember when last we had done missionary — a massive tick in the 'try more positions'-box. Therapist helped by introducing more techniques and tips and opening my mind to things like cunnilingus which I was not keen on my husband performing before. Therapy as a whole cleared out a lot of the "pollution" that I had in my mind surrounding sex, which aided me in crossing those hurdles and embracing new experiences by letting myself go and enjoy what sex had to offer.

The most significant change that losing weight has brought into our bedroom was self-confidence. I feel confident in my skin. I feel confident naked. I have no problem being or being seen nude. I have no hesitation in letting my husband touch me, look at me or kiss me in any way he wants to. I do not feel that I want to hide from him or stop him. I welcome the attention — I crave it. I love it when my husband looks at me as someone to be desired when he cannot keep his hands off me or his mouth off mine. After years of not being a sexy wife, I completely embrace it now and enjoy every minute of it.

In June 2020, I went for an endometrial ablation, which completely stopped my menstruation. Suddenly it was 'play time' all the time! Perhaps an ablation was something I should've had done many years ago? Maybe even directly after my youngest was born? But I had always been so obese and never considered a good candidate for any surgery. I am thankful for losing weight and having options like these in my life now. I think so often, just being able to have surgery without a whole string of weight-related complications tagging along is a privilege not recognised by many.

Today I am proud of our sex life. We experiment with many sexual techniques and continuously improve our sexual intelligence. We've tried and been successful at things like

Multiple female orgasms.
Female orgasm via penetration only.
Simultaneous male and female orgasms.
Full body orgasms — a personal favourite.
Oral sex as our main sexual course.
Orgasms through oral sex only.
Multiple male orgasms etc.

Currently, we are experimenting with nipple orgasms. There is always a new goal or technique that we are keen on trying. We keep improving and growing and, most importantly, enjoying each other and having fun. We both have stressful and busy lives, but sex is our way just to be, let go and enjoy. Yes, sex is not everything nor the most important thing. In our case, it adds a beautiful richness to our marriage and is something special that we both enjoy immensely. My husband makes me feel like the sexiest woman alive. In response, I believe I very definitely make him feel like the luckiest man. I think we're doing exceptionally well for a marriage of nearly seventeen years with four children.

In February 2021, I sent the same friend a birthday message to congratulate her on her fortieth birthday.

She messaged me back, "Thank you! Now we are very old!"

"No, no, no! We are not going down that route again. I don't feel my age at all," I jested back.

Fighting The Fear Of Regaining

I used to think of reaching my goal weight as gaining entry to that magical place where everything would suddenly be easy, and I would be happy forever and ever. A mantra often shared in the weight loss community is, "Being fat is hard. Losing weight is hard. Pick your hard." This mantra makes it sound like being thin and remaining thin is easy. I have said it before, and I will repeat it. Nothing could be further from the truth.

Yes, I had reached my goal weight. I had experienced both being fat — that was hard — and losing weight — and that too was hard. And what then? I was supposed to reach that magical place where everything was easy and intuitive, only it wasn't. It was still hard! I was so scared I would lose the plot and yo-yo, regaining all eighty kilograms.

I voiced this fear to others; some felt that the fear was justified and should exist to maintain my weight loss successfully. Most thought that I had nothing to worry about, and if I just continued with my eating plan and exercising religiously, all would be well — in other words, I had to continue to be perfect. Some felt that I should discard all diets and my scale and eat intuitively. None of these opinions made me fear regaining less.

The fear of regaining and my obsession with the number on the scale was stealing from me. It was stealing from my happiness and carefreeness; constantly fearing to regain hampered me from enjoying my new weight and body. Being so scared to put a foot wrong made me feel unworthy. For example, if my husband were to ask me if I'd also like a sweet, a snack, a cookie, or whatever treat we bought on the odd occasion that we did purchase something usually not allowed to eat, then I would always reply with: "No, I do not deserve it." That was what this desire to always be a perfect weight was stealing from me!

During our last session, Therapist asked, "Explain to me the process of how you would regain eighty kilograms."

What a counter-intuitive question to ask — my goal was not to regain my weight, yet here was Therapist asking me to explain to him how I would achieve it. Yet, the question also made perfect sense. To diffuse fear, one needs to understand what exactly it is that you are fearing.

"Well ... It would start with me just gaining a kilogram, perhaps even two. I would try to lose those kilos, but I would not be able to. And that gain would become three kilograms and then four. Eventually, I will get to a point where I refuse to weigh myself. I would feel like I had been trying everything to lose the gained kilos, but nothing worked. I would give up and let myself go and spiral out of control," I answered.

"Was a number on the scale the only thing that you gained from losing weight?" he asked. "Did all your efforts to lose weight and the entire weight loss journey you've been on produce only a number on the scale that you can show off proudly and say, 'Look, I've lost eighty kilograms! The number on the scale is the reward for my efforts.' When I listen to your explanation of how you will regain your weight, I only hear you worrying about this number on the scale. Is that the only thing that you have to lose from regaining?"

Sometimes someone else has to point out the absurdity of our argument to us, as we are too blind to see it ourselves!

Of course, a number on the scale was not my only reward. I gained greater self-confidence, a more active lifestyle. I had more energy and enjoyed life more. I now have the opportunity to experiment with clothes and styles that were previously not an option. I have finally discovered my authentic self and a sparkling personality before hidden under layers of fat. I was no longer hiding. I lived my life to the fullest and grabbed every opportunity that came my way. I even have this fantastic opportunity via my blog to help other people. My weight loss had indirectly given me more purpose in my life.

But for some reason, when I thought of what I would lose by regaining, I could only think of that number on the scale. While losing weight, many of us fixate on that number and the pace it goes down. It is tunnel vision. After a while, the number on the scale becomes the only thing at the end of the tunnel. We lose sight of what else we gain on our journey through that tunnel.

"When I listen to you describing how you would regain your weight, I hear a familiar story. The same story a gambling addict would tell about how gambling sucked him in repeatedly. Everything would be going well while his winnings are increasing, but when he starts to lose, he keeps trying to win back what he lost — usually without success. The obsession with winning would eventually cost him everything."

"Hmm," I said as I pondered this metaphor.

In the one scenario, the "game" is to gamble, and the game's objective is to make money. The measure of success is the total amount of winnings, and losing control happens when you keep losing more money despite your best efforts to try and win back what you've lost.

In the other scenario, the "game" is to diet, and the game's objective is the number on the scale. The measure of success is the total amount of weight lost, and losing control occurs when you keep gaining weight despite your best efforts to eat healthily and exercise.

If you look at both scenarios using the objectives above, they are doomed to fail. It is impossible to always win when gambling. And it is impossible to always have the perfect weight on the scale, especially if you also desire to live.

"Yes, I can see how the two scenarios are similar," I added. "But I am not sure how that helps me with my fear of regaining?"

"Well, another way to gamble is not for the sake of winning. You could gamble merely for the entertainment value while setting limits on both the amount of time and money you are willing to spend. If your allotted time runs out and you have won something, that is great. If you have lost money, then it is also fine as you've experienced entertainment value from the time and money you have spent," Therapist tried to explain it as simply as possible.

"I don't understand. If I gain weight, then I have lost! I don't win anything if I gain weight. I cannot play the game for another reason while having peace with the number on the scale. I need to keep track and focus on that number on the scale." I replied.

"You need to search for other reasons to play. In your case, you can play for fitness or to feel better about yourself and how you look. Search for the other reasons," Therapist tried to elaborate.

"Okay," I said, but I didn't completely grasp the concept yet. This type of thing, where I needed time to go home and work through something myself, often happened in sessions. However, that session was our last. I knew I could contact Therapist afterwards for more clarity if I could still not figure it out, but I didn't want to. I was so much in thought about everything we discussed that I almost forgot to take my handbag before heading home. I tend to overthink, and when I am brewing, I am very careless.

That evening I tried to explain the metaphor to my husband, but my inadequate explanation didn't convince him that this was a solution to my fear of regaining. I did not explain it very well, but I did not fully understand it myself yet.

I tried to make sense of it in this way. You can gamble just for the fun of it until your time or money runs out. You do not worry about whether you've lost or won anything; you would constantly be winning because you would be winning entertainment. Gambling for entertainment is a way to turn the gambling scenario into one where you would always win. You do not fear the value of your winnings, as you are not playing for money.

Looking at the dieting scenario, I had to find something else to diet for other than the number on the scale. I considered my 'other reason to play', perhaps the way that I look. I was also not sure what will run out in the dieting scenario. In the gambling scenario, it was either time or money. But dieting should be for life. A diet that you cannot follow for the rest of your life is not sustainable. So perhaps it is time that should be running out? My metaphor looked something like this. I diet for how I look until time runs out without worrying about the scale anymore. However, I could not see how I would have won, regardless of what the scale said at the end of the time. If the number on the scale had increased significantly, I would've lost. I needed to worry about the number on the scale.

Drawing a parallel between the gambling and dieting scenarios was a highly complex plot for me to unravel. How does one turn the dieting game into one where you do not have to fear the number on the scale because you will always be a winner regardless of that number? I could not see the answer to this question.

Therapy is nothing but a bunch of "A-ha!"-moments strung together, and a few days later, it hit me right between the eyes. I had the game wrong! Therapist was not referring to the dieting game. That was not the game I was supposed to play or continue playing. The game I was supposed to be playing was eating healthy and sensibly and exercising — the game of leading a healthy life.

I reworded my healthy life version of the gambling metaphor to sound like this. Even when the scale does not reflect your efforts, eating a healthy, well-balanced diet and exercising will always benefit you. You will find the rewards in other areas, such as improving the way you look, your fitness level, or your general health. If you choose to play the game of eating well and exercising, you will always be a winner.

Over my first year of maintaining my goal weight, I ran more than one-thousand-five-hundred kilometres and attended just less than eighty Pilates classes, but I've not seen any difference on the scale. I could feel the difference in my clothes and my energy levels and definitely in how I looked. I've won! Even if the scale would like me to believe that I didn't.

It is challenging for someone who actively tries to lose weight to ignore the scale entirely. But actively looking out for the other benefits to leading a healthy life is crucial to ongoing motivation and not becoming despondent when the scale does not reflect your efforts.

Has this view helped me fight the fear of regaining?

If I have to be honest, I will probably always fear regaining. But this view has helped me immensely in living with that fear in the whole-somest way possible. I now obsess over the scale a whole lot less than what I used to. I focus my efforts on living the healthiest and most active life I can, and I believe that doing this will always benefit me. I have also decided to stop weighing at my Weigh-Less group as I do not need the additional fear that I will go over the two-kilogram limit from my goal weight. I now keep myself wholly accountable.

I try to control my emotional triggers, particularly those that cause me to eat compulsively and scream at my children. I achieve this by being highly self-aware. When I find myself where I feel I might lose it, I try to remove myself from that situation before I react. It is not easy, not easy at all. I try not to get to the point where life feels impossible and that no matter what I do, I cannot win — because impossible feels like going home and eating.

Every single morning when I wake up before my feet touch the ground, I tell myself, "Today is going to be a good day." Many days are good, but I still have bad days where I overreact or eat what I am not supposed to eat or binge on something that is just too good to pass up. I guess that is life? When that happens, I put it behind me as soon as possible, not letting a bad snack become a bad meal, day, week, month or year.

Getting Away With Obesity

Whenever I see an obese person, I want to walk up to them and introduce myself. I want to tell them that I lost eighty kilos, show them photos of what I used to look like, and then show them what I look like now. I want to give them hope.

But I do not do any of the above.

Instead, I watch them walk away and hope that, in some way, they will find their way to me. I am too afraid of insulting them. Perhaps they are currently trying to lose weight, and my observations will make them feel even more vulnerable or a failure?

I once made the mistake of approaching a new school mum about her weight, which backfired completely. Maybe I mishandled it, but she responded to my introduction with a lengthy medical explanation of why she cannot lose weight. I do not want to be yet another person she feels she needs to explain her story. I want to be the person who brings her hope and a feeling that she is not alone.

There is never a good reason to comment upon someone else's weight. If you want to say something, the best thing you can say is, "You look fantastic." Anything else is considered unacceptable. If someone wants to talk about losing weight, they will. It is a "Don't call us, we'll call you"-situation.

Right?

And so we get away with it. Poor obese people! Always body shamed. Always victims of society's beauty expectations.

It is time to wake up! Please, wake up and acknowledge your addiction. No one is going to organise an intervention for you. No one wants to be guilty of body shaming someone they love. No one wants to hurt the already frail ego of an obese person. Loved ones organise interventions for alcohol, drug and gambling addicts, well-meaning friends and family wishing to address real problems. Hardly anyone sees food addiction as a real problem — it is hardly even recognised as an addiction.

But it is a real problem!

What will convince you that I had a real problem? Would you believe my predicament was severe if I told you that I could not visit some public bathroom stalls because I couldn't fit onto the toilet despite fitting through the stall door sideways? Even the toilet at my own home posed a problem for me. It has a wall on one side and a raised bath on the other side. I could not fit onto the loo at home when I was at my heaviest! When I was a teenager, my arms were already too short to go around my backside to wipe my bum. Consequently, I would wipe from the front. That became a habit, and I still find myself doing that and then needing to wash afterwards.

I see quite an amount of free support out there for addicts in the form of Narcotics or Alcoholics Anonymous meetings and support structures. Overeaters have Overeaters Anonymous, but it is not very well known. The first time I read about it was during research for this book. How is it that in more than thirty years of being morbidly obese, no one has ever shared Overeaters Anonymous' details with me? That even after losing eighty kilograms and finding myself searching for ways to keep that weight off, I had still not heard about the program. The first time anyone ever told me he could see that I needed help was when a therapist suggested I come for therapy. He saw my need for support without ever seeing me in person. He saw it purely by the amount of shame I was carrying with me.

I feel that the support for food addiction is not the same as what is available for other addictions. The Weigh-Less program I used for my weight loss also has weekly group meetings, but it is a paid-for program. Once you have reached your goal weight, you become a life member, but you have to remain within two kilograms of your goal weight; otherwise, you are out of the club. Not literally, but you have to start paying again to attend meetings.

Instead of looking at their compulsive eating and emotional problems, people try to solve obesity by dieting. Even reality TV game shows such as *The Biggest Loser* illustrate how to "solve" a weight loss problem through diet and exercise. Mental and emotional issues receive very little attention when trying to lose weight. Would anyone have found a reality TV game show with a group of narcotic addicts to be acceptable? Of course not! Yet, obese people trying to recover from their illnesses and being put on display while doing that in a competition to see who can do it best is acceptable?

The dieting industry has become a massive money-making industry. One of my pet peeves is when people ask how to eat correctly, and in answer to their questions, commentators refer to a dietitian, weight loss program, exercise program, a commercial diet. I get it that these are people's jobs. I understand that diets are copyright protected. I do not share any of the specifics on the Weigh-Less eating program I followed for the same reason and because I do not want my message to be associated with any specific diet. I genuinely do not care what diet you are trying to follow, but it remains tough to see someone struggling and not help with an excellent free resource for some primary food education. Such a resource does not exist as everyone disagrees over what it means to eat correctly. The disagreements increase with every new diet promulgated.

Every single person believes that their diet or program is the best. A compulsive eating problem is probably the most difficult of all addictions to solve. We need to eat to live. We cannot simply withdraw from food. In addition, we cannot simply cut out certain problematic food groups from our lives. For the diets where I have tried, for example, to cut carbohydrates, I would merely start overeating eggs and peanut butter to address my carbohydrate cravings. A diet that treats any particular food group as the culprit has never worked for me. I'd always overeat on something else.

Society does not treat obesity and compulsive eating with the same concern as other addictions because fat people continue to be regular community members. We go to our jobs, raise our children and pay our taxes. As far as possible, we continue our everyday lives, all the while just being fat. Our addiction steals from our health and feelings of self-worth but doesn't burden the community at large, except perhaps via our loved ones' concern for our well-being. Even then, people view a husband commenting on his wife's weight as a bad thing. A husband should accept his wife just the way she is because he loves her, right?

When I was still young and in school, my peers teased me relentlessly because of my weight. I was also excluded from many social circles and had hardly any friends. My self-image has been broken down throughout my entire life — in my home, at school, at university. Whichever platform or place I found myself to be physically present in my self-image suffered. I am still trying to rebuild my feelings of worthiness. I remember one particular incident. I was thirteen and had just finished primary school. That year over December, I attended a church camp for pupils on their way to high school. One of the activities we did at this camp was a self-improvement activity. We each had a paper pinned to the back of our shirt. Our teammates would take turns to write down an optional complement and something to improve on. The idea was for these to be anonymous, of course. Someone wrote on my paper that I would be a more pleasant person if I could manage to lose some weight. I remember that sentence still to this day. I was already an ugly person physically, but I also had an unattractive personality because of my weight.

I don't believe incidents such as this one are acceptable. And when I tell it now, people react with shock: "How was behaviour like that acceptable at a church camp? Someone should've talked to that group about things not to say to their peers." Kids are brutally honest — and perhaps that is a good thing — but while raising them, we try to tame that honesty out.

"Stop pointing fingers!"

"Don't mention other people's disabilities."

"Don't talk so loudly!"

"That is not a nice thing to say."

"Don't call someone fat."

And then we end up in a society where fat becomes socially acceptable. There is never a good reason for anyone to comment about someone else's weight. And if you do, then you are body shaming. It is wrong to body shame. We do not want to hurt anyone's feelings. But behind closed doors or in small huddles, it is the topic of choice, and we DO shame people and comment on their weight. There are also keyboard warriors from behind the safety of the internet, like what happened when I posted my boudoir photos taken to celebrate my eighty kilograms weight loss and people commented on the appearance of my tummy.

My husband loves me, and he never wants to hurt my feelings, and because he sees how much I beat myself up over what I eat, if I were to tell him now that I had an insatiable craving, for example, for cheesecake, he would go out and buy some for me. He would do this because he wouldn't want to make me feel judged and because he wants to see me happy. I can also assure you that my husband would be okay with me picking up all eighty kilograms again. He might, somewhere along the way, comment on my weight gain, but because he feels that it is not his place to comment on my weight, he would be more likely just to let me be. That is what society expects of him. His parents and the community raised him to be that type of man.

Some of the therapy coursework I did focused on body image. A specific exercise we've tried was the following:

Take a photograph of yourself, as naked as you feel comfortable.
Print it out.
Mark all your flaws with a black marker.

On mine, I have marked excess skin with which I am still not happy, too wide thighs and calves, stretch marks, scars from my four C-sections and hernia operation, boobs that are too small and so on. I also marked non-physical things like my body rejecting our first baby, years of yo-yo dieting and struggling with hernias.

I felt terrible after this exercise. I was demotivated and wondered what the use of losing eighty kilograms was if I can still not see myself as pretty? Then I might as well quit trying and enjoy the vitality and freedom of movement now while it still lasts before I pick up the weight again. But I also realised, in this thought process, that losing weight meant so much more to me than just cosmetics. The fruit of weight loss lie far more profound than outward appearances.

For the second part of the exercise, I had to give an unmarked photo to my husband on which he was supposed to write what he liked about my body. The idea was for me to look at his kind words, accept them and make them my own. My husband just circled the area where my heart is and said that that was the prettiest part. What I look like has never mattered to him. Extremely sweet and precisely the response that a good husband should have. It also confirms my concern that he will allow me to let myself go if I once again find myself powerless to my addiction and too far down the rabbit hole to be able to turn back.

When should what we look like matter? I don't believe it ever should, but I feel this way because of the silent judgment from people judging books by their covers. The preconceived notion that fat people are dumb, lazy, uninteresting is what I reject. Does what we look like matter when we cannot fit onto a toilet anymore? Of course, it does! Even before we get to that point, it already matters. I wish there were an acceptable way to help overeaters like myself by raising these concerns respectfully. But I am afraid that we are going the other way on this. We embrace fat, are too scared to approach someone with a weight problem, and in general, we turn a blind eye.

I have specifically asked my husband to speak up when he sees I am losing the plot. My expectation is not that he starts calling me fat. I expect him to speak up when he sees I react to my emotional triggers by overeating and that he will help me mature emotionally. I teach him about "me" by asking him to watch my videos and read my writings.

But what if I decide to overeat in secret now, not wanting anyone to catch me out? I cannot expect him to be my eating compass forever, either. Ultimately, I am fighting this maintenance battle on my own.

Eighty Kilos of Shame

The First Step

It is not the mountain we conquer but ourselves.
— Sir Edmund Hillary

When I meet up with people to discuss their weight problems, I like to leave them with a plan of action or at least know that they have enough information on how to do the next right thing. Deciding on such an action plan or first step is not easy — just talking to me was already a massive step for them to take. I get confused looks and questions when I ask what they are planning to do next.

"How do I know which diet to choose?"
"Should I join a gym?"
"Do I need to exercise initially?"
"Can I start on my own?"
"What if I fail again? I have never been able to stick to a diet!"
"How do I start?"
"How do I bring myself to start?"
Or the most baffling one:
"What do you mean I need to do something? Can I not just be aware of my problem?"

All these questions speak of fear for the task that lies ahead. It is one thing to realise that you need to do something, but another thing entirely to put action to your needs. Sometimes the task in front of us seems so massive that we give up before we've even begun.

Not being able to start is a mental block. It is a massive mental block! Mentally the journey up the colossal mountain ahead seems so complicated and so daunting that just thinking about what that first step should be is impossible — let alone taking that first step.

I understand a few of the reasons for this procrastination, and I want to share them here, hoping it will help someone get started.

The first reason is the anticipated effort of what it will be like to undertake this journey up the mountain. It feels like it will be a lot of pain and hard work — that is probably true. But when comparing the expected pain of the journey forward to the pain they currently find themselves in, the journey ahead seems to be more troublesome. Why would they put themselves through more trouble if they can be okay just continuing the way they've done up to now?

People feel like this because they cannot imagine what it will be like once they've reached their destination. Some, like myself, have never weighed a "normal" weight. They have no frame of reference to understand how that would be. I have so much empathy for this.

I would ask the person sitting across from me to explain what they hope to see at the top of the mountain. What are the reasons that they want to lose weight? I expect that fully understanding and voicing out or even listing why they want to lose weight can help them dream and visualise. I can also explain what losing weight has done for me, hoping to somehow sketch that scene on top for them.

Sometimes, despite my best efforts to help them imagine what losing weight would be like, I still get the feeling that people do not believe themselves to be worthy of experiencing that. They do not see reaching their goal weight as their destiny. I was like this as well. I also needed a reason to start, showing me how it would be beneficial to someone else. I started my therapy journey because I thought that somehow it would be helpful for my husband to have a less easily triggered and angry wife. I started my weight loss journey because I didn't want my children to grow up with memories of me struggling with hernias. I grew up with my mum struggling immensely.

Both scenarios worked out well for me, so I cannot write that these reasons were incorrect. I can testify that my commitment to both journeys increased a hundredfold once I started seeing the benefits there were for myself. Only then, I truly began believing that I was travelling these journeys for myself and was worthy of reaping the rewards at the end for my win.

When someone expressed that they didn't consider themselves worthy of losing weight, I did not know what to do or say. How do you explain to the stranger sitting across from you that they are deserving and that they should show themselves the self-love needed? I forgot that I also once considered myself unworthy and that I, at one stage, didn't love myself. Unworthiness is tricky to identify as nobody initially comes out with the whole sack of potatoes. The lack of self-love is present in how they talk about themselves, how people close to them treat them, and why they want to lose weight. When I notice the lack of self-love, I try to work on how losing weight will benefit the people close to them, hoping that these benefits would get them to start as it did for me.

Weight loss is not sustainable if you want to lose weight for anybody else. Eating healthily and exercising are both acts of self-love. Starting a self-improvement journey, such as a journey to lose eighty kilograms, requires a declaration that states, "I am worth starting this. I love myself enough to do this for myself." Sometimes, self-love is not there, and you have to work with whatever you have at your disposal. Furthermore, I think I just had another "A-ha"-moment in understanding why Therapist played the 'husband card' to get me to start therapy. He was doing what was necessary to get me going, which is what I precisely do now for other people.

Something unique for me to witness is that point where self-love kicks in. You can see how someone begins to shine. You notice how personal grooming improves and how confidence increases. There is a sparkle in the eye and an increase in energy that was never there before. You can also see how the person becomes worthy and is no longer just an afterthought. Few things give me greater pleasure than bearing witness to this part of the transformation.

Finally, the most significant reason I see for people not wanting to take that first step is the sheer enormity of the task ahead. They imagine that they need to lose all of their excess weight at once, and because that is incomprehensible, they give up before even starting.

Fortunately, this is also the most straightforward rock in the road to roll out of the way. The task that lies ahead is always a concrete concept. It is not dependent on the individual, their personality, emotions or any other abstract subject. It is purely a piece of work, and there is always a logical way to break down a job into smaller, less daunting parts. The only way to eat an elephant is bit by bit, right?

I never lost eighty kilograms. I lost eight kilograms ten times.

I never just started and ran ten kilometres. I first walked for thirty minutes, then walked and ran certain sections, then ran just more than three kilometres, then five kilometres and so on.

I never once felt that I had to do absolutely everything all at once.

Sometimes, it is unclear to someone how to break a task into smaller, manageable sections. If this is the case, someone with a more objective and detached view can help. Our Weigh-Less group leaders always break down the total amount of weight to lose into ten steps. Your group leader gives these ten steps to you on your first day of joining and emphasises focussing on each step. The ten-step program is your first logical breakdown of the task that lies ahead.

This method creates the opportunity for continuous motivation by acknowledging each milestone. I made a point of celebrating every step along the journey to losing weight. Sometimes I would buy a new dress or a pair of earrings. Sometimes my husband and I would go out for the evening to celebrate. I found these mini celebrations to be vital so as not to reach that gloomy feeling of, "I am never going to be able to reach the top of the mountain."

Ultimately, to accomplish anything in life, you have to start. Procrastination will not help you achieve anything. In addition to being the most critical step, that first step is often the hardest to take.

Young Food Addicts

"At least I don't drink, do drugs, or smoke. I simply overeat!"

The above is a story I often hear from strangers who message me. It is as if they want to say that overeating is the least of the evils, and imply they are better of trapped in the maze of overeating than in some other maze. Perhaps this is true? Maybe of all the addictions out there, being addicted to food is the better addiction to have? It is still an addiction, though. Softening it by making it appear less than other addictions doesn't make it any less of one.

I define addiction as the continuous and repetitive quest to soothe your feelings and increase your Dopamine levels via an external substance or action that makes you feel good. Later on, using this external substance or activity becomes the only way to reach that place where you feel good about yourself.

Why become addicted to food, though? The amount of food you need to eat to feel better is considerable — one piece of chocolate does not have the same effect as the entire slab. Your substance quantity required for a dopamine increase is much less with other substances, like drugs and alcohol. Why choose food? Why would so many people become addicted to food?

Perhaps food is just the more accessible option? You do not need a dealer for your fix; you go to your local supermarket. Food production and the availability of food is of utmost importance in society. There always must be food.

Perhaps food is the more socially acceptable option? You are supposed to eat. How else will you live? A healthy appetite is a sign of good health. Others expect you to eat and relish what you eat at social gatherings. Someone who enjoys their food is often considered jolly, likeable, and upbeat.

Perhaps there was no option other than food? That would undoubtedly be the case if the addiction started in childhood. A child cannot become addicted — or is highly unlikely to become addicted — to drugs and alcohol. What option other than food would be available for a child looking for something to help them self-soothe?

Because I grew up as an obese child, I naturally assumed that my weight problems were genetic or related to my poor food upbringing. Being a mum of four children taught me that children eat by instinct and need. You cannot make them eat their food when they are not hungry — when they are not hungry, they are indeed not hungry. They will also undoubtedly let you know when they are hungry by crying as babies or strongly verbalising it when older. If we pass fat down generations genetically, why then, in my case, does it seem like the genes suddenly stopped with me? Certainly, at least one of my four children should have been overweight? But none of them is? Each one of them is a healthy weight.

When I considered food as something to become addicted to and my newly discovered emotional eating triggers, it started making sense to me that perhaps in some way, I had been addicted to food from a very young age. I am not sure exactly when my weight problem started. I have a 'not overweight'-photo of myself when I was three years old. So my weight problem must have started somewhere between the ages three and five because I was already overweight by the time I went to school at age six.

When I presented the concept of being a young food addict on my blog, the reception was lukewarm, and my blog followers did not seem convinced. I did not see any evidence of using food to soothe their emotions amongst my children. I am also not privy to the patterns of other children who might already be a bit overweight. Nor had I heard anyone mention something like mindless compulsive eating for children until one particular day.

I have a good friend who is also overweight, and we discuss weight often. Almost every time I talk to her, the topic of choice comes up. She is not in denial over her obesity status. She is forever on some form of diet, just about to start a new diet, or has just picked up fifteen kilos. I badly want to help her, but losing weight is one topic where you can only offer an ear and some insight. In the same way, you cannot gain weight for someone else; you cannot lose weight for that person either.

On one occasion, my friend invited me to her house for coffee. I love visiting her. She is a fascinating person, and we usually end up chatting for hours. Despite her struggles, she has a great depth of understanding of weight issues, and she keeps me forever humble on what it means to struggle with one's weight. On this occasion, however, she had a crucial and pressing issue that she wanted to discuss.

She asked: "Did you always find exercising to be easy or something that you enjoy?"

"Uhm — no, not initially. Initially, it sucked," I said. "It was a long time before I started enjoying it."

Recalling a prior experience, she said, "Yes, that is how I remember it as well. Once a friend and I went to the gym together. It was torture in the beginning, but as we got fitter, we both started enjoying it."

"Why do you want to know?" I asked, thinking that she perhaps wanted to take up exercising again. She is usually starting something new, so that wouldn't have surprised me, but this didn't feel like an important topic to discuss in person. I had the feeling there was more to come.

"I want to see if I can get my son to start exercising. I've started him this week with some exercises we received from the school, but he does not enjoy them. I was hoping I could see him through the first few weeks, and then he'll start enjoying them," she answered.

Unfortunately, my friend's son is an overweight young teenager about my eldest's age. Sighing deeply, I responded, "Ah, but there is a big difference to address here first. I wanted to start exercising. A few years ago, you wanted to start going to the gym. But you are now deciding for your son to start exercising. Of course, there is going to be resistance. Why do you feel that he should start exercising?"

"I have to do something!" she exclaimed.

Puzzled and sensing her helplessness, I asked: "What is it that you feel that you need to do?"

"I need to help my son lose weight. He has a big problem. And I cannot seem to solve his problem with a diet. I also do not want to put him on a diet. I had been placed on diets since I was nine. I don't want that for him as well," she replied with frustration.

The Christmas holidays were less than a month before this, and she continued, explaining her problem, "Over the holidays, I've started worrying about him even more. Let me tell you this story; then perhaps you will understand. We bought a big box of cookies to enjoy while the schools were closed. Between me, my husband and our son, it should've lasted us the entire duration of the holiday. On Christmas Day, we opened the box, and each had about two cookies. A few days later, I wanted to set out some more cookies for us, but I could not find the box of cookies anywhere. I looked everywhere; I asked everyone. No one knew where the cookies were. It is only the three of us in this house; there was no one else. Someone must've known something."

"Yes, that is strange. Have you since discovered what happened to the box of cookies?" I asked.

"Yes, I have. Eventually, I found the empty box, with a few other empty treat packets hidden in one of my son's drawers," she replied with utmost frustration and defeat.

"That must've been a shocking discovery," I said. "What was your reaction when you found the empty box?"

"I did what any mum would do. I gave him an earful. I told him that we do so many things to help him. I try to keep enough nice eats in the house so he does not feel that those spoils are scarce and that he has to overindulge when someone presents him with treats. I try to prepare healthy food for him to eat. I try to get him to exercise. I try so hard! And then he goes and does something like this," she answered.

"Have you tried asking him why he ate the cookies?"

"I did," she replied, "After my initial reprimanding, I thought I should state my concerns calmly. So, thinking of your emotional eating video, I tried to enquire about the emotions that caused him to eat the entire box of cookies. But I got the typical 'I don't know why I did it'-answer."

My friend described something that I have been searching for for a long time. I was finally hearing someone else's testimony of young food addiction, and it was giving me goosebumps because of its familiar feeling. I had been guilty of this myself! My friend was busy describing a young Mart-Mari. In her narrative of compulsive eating performed by a child, followed by shame over what happened, I could see myself.

Her son ate that entire box of cookies, which should've lasted them for the duration of the holidays, and a few other packets of treats. He felt a need to get the cookies packed away somewhere for the next time and then eat, presumably inhaling all the cookies in the box. My friend's son is a child growing up in a house where treats are readily available. He is not starved of treats. He could have perhaps even gotten something else to eat, but he decided that he required that box of cookies. He realised what he did was wrong and tried to hide the evidence in his drawer. When confronted with how the cookies had disappeared, he lied about it, heaping more shame onto himself. He hoped that his mum would not discover the empty box, and when she did and confronted him with the proof, he could not give her an answer. Most likely, he doesn't even know why he ate the cookies. He knew that his conduct was wrong and wanted to keep his behaviour a secret.

That is the sad and all too familiar burden of food addiction. It is ludicrous and nonsensical, but at that moment, when you need to eat, nothing feels silly about your actions. I did it. Sometimes I still find myself doing it. It is a vicious cycle, as guilt over what you ate causes you to want to eat more. It becomes an impossible pattern to break. And as a child, you do not have it within your means to escape your addiction.

How I Found Myself In The Maze

In December 2019, I found myself at the end of an eighty kilograms weight loss journey, wondering just where I could find some glue to secure this tiny marble. Or wondering if there is perhaps something that I can do to ensure that neither myself nor anyone else bumps or rocks the maze and hits the marble out of its place.

So much information is out there on how to lose weight; it is overwhelming. Yet, there is scant information on maintaining a considerable weight loss. The most popular view on weight loss maintenance is that it is impossible. Once a fattie, always a fattie.

Realising that I cannot rely on solely my strong willpower, but not having had a chance yet to discuss this with Therapist, I started to blog. In my very first blog post, when I still knew nothing, I asked these questions:

> "If you are a person of 'normal' weight reading this, I'd like to ask you this: How do thin people stay thin? Do you ever consider your diet? Do you ever weigh yourself? And if you do, how often? I come from an overweight family, and all I've ever known is how to be fat ..."

I have since come to realise that the one group of people, the people I view as never having struggled with their weight and the other group of people, ex-fatties like myself, do not play the same game. I am resting in a hollow space, waiting for life to knock me out again. They are not in a maze at all. The weight loss field is not one they have ever needed to navigate. I started my maintenance journey by asking the wrong questions. Even the right answers to the wrong questions do not mean anything to your problem. Instead, I should have asked:

"How did I get in the maze in the first place?"

I walked into the weight loss maze when I was very young. I was lost. I was hurt. I didn't know what to do, so I did the only thing I knew helped a little bit. I ate! And, somehow, that made things both better and worse all at the same time.

In my life story, I can see that I've started using food as a drug from when I was still a very young child. I thought my case was exceptional as I never really saw this pattern in other children. My friend's story made me realise that my narrative is not unique. There are probably hundreds of thousands of similar cases out there with parents who cannot recognise it. Or maybe even sitting with their hands in their hair as to how to solve their children's weight problems — or perhaps having accepted the inevitable that their children are the recipients of their overweight genes and they can not do anything about it.

I believe fat can flow from one generation to the next — but I do not see it happen genetically. I see the problem lying in the creation of a breeding ground for food addiction. What makes this breeding ground particularly fertile is:

Making food seem like a solution to our emotional hurt and shame, and in creating reasons for that emotional hurt and shame to be there — i.e., creating unhealthy coping mechanisms.

The first part to understanding this 'food as a drug'-behaviour in children lies in the awareness of the messages we communicate regarding food. Some of the information that adults, not just parents, communicate regarding food is pleasure, love, joy and community.

When we are good, we or someone else reward us with something nice to eat. We associate food, usually in abundance, with celebrations and good times. Grandparents are synonymous with treats, and it is socially acceptable, actually expected, for grandparents to love their grandchildren by spoiling them with treats. Over holidays we fill our cookie tins. And when year-end reports go out, even the school suggests treating the children with ice cream for their hard work.

In my childhood home, treats were not in abundance. Our diet was primarily monotonous, lacking balance and very similar from day to day, meals consisting of starches and other cheap staples. We had enough to eat and were never hungry. An abundance of tasty dishes and special meals indicated that we had money and could buy treats or have guests over for a change. Guests also implied that my mum would be on her best behaviour for almost an entire day and would probably not shout at me.

Along with the pleasure and uplifting properties we assign to certain foods, I find a gap in education around the nutritional value of food. Around our dinner table, I try to explain that protein builds muscles, that carbohydrates fuel our bodies and why we need minerals and vitamins. I also explain that specific vitamins are fat-soluble and that our bodies can only absorb those vitamins when taken with fat. Yet, I feel I am explaining the bare essentials and that my children still have considerable gaps in their food education. But I also feel alone in this battle. My perception, which might be selective because I am unaware of what other families are doing, is that food education is not a priority and that what I am doing is rare. I almost solely see the 'food as pleasure'-messages.

If we assign so many pleasureful and uplifting properties to food, to me, it makes a tremendous amount of sense that a child looking for something to help them self-soothe would turn towards food. What other options are there? And it is so easily accessible!

But why would a child need to look for something through which to self-soothe? Well, why wouldn't they? Children are also human, with normal human emotions. We even teach babies to self-soothe. It is one of the primary factors in getting them to sleep through at night. Certain people, and children, are more in need of this. Is this perhaps a personality trait passed down through the generations?

The emotions they are trying to numb can be small, like being alone, bored, or possibly traumatic or sad. I also think it is understandable for a child to desire to hide their behaviour. I was an expert at hiding that which I ate in secret. I would take as little as possible so that my behaviour would go unnoticed. I would drink extra milk or eat leftover bread or whatever else of substance I could find in our cupboard. Or perhaps something that my mum hardly ever used, such as custard powder. I am still an expert at making microwave custard — extra sweet. I knew that if my mum were to find out about it, I would be in a lot of trouble. She often did find out. Yet all her reprimanding did was make me want to eat more.

Writing about reprimand brings me to the second part of understanding' food as a drug' behaviour. When we react with anger and accusations, all we do is pile on shame. The receiver seldom interprets the message as 'I did something wrong.' Instead, we hear: 'I am wrong' — even when that was not the intention. We then internalise these messages, store them, and they become our internal voice.

Using our internal voice and telling ourselves these messages are even worse. I tried to explain to a friend of mine, the same one who accused me of going into my schoolgirl mode, why I find it so incredibly difficult to weigh myself less often. At one stage, I told her, "I know I shouldn't weigh myself like this. I am sorry. I am terrible."

She stopped me almost right away to explain that I am not a terrible person, "You sometimes feeling that you need to weigh yourself every day does not make you a terrible person. Perhaps what you are trying is not right, but it still doesn't make you a bad person. All you are doing by saying that you are a terrible person is to pile more shame on yourself."

She explained this by an example of eating a piece of chocolate cake. Whenever she decides to have a chocolate cake piece, she enjoys every last bite of it. She tells herself she will not feel guilty or bad about having the cake, because as she explained to me, "The only thing that guilt or shame over a piece of chocolate cake causes is more chocolate cake!"

And is that not the truth? Shame causes us to feel that: We are wrong. We are never going to get this right. We might as well give up.

I see us passing fat down generations like this. We almost solely build pleasure around food. The food we find pleasurable is not the healthy and nutritious types of food, but often the very refined, processed, or sugary types of food. We also neglect proper food and nutrition education because we often don't know ourselves. Along with the glorification of food in our lives, we also pass down the shame. Be that in overreacting, mentioning something that our children already feel self-conscious about, or even trying to perfect them and adding unnecessary pressure. Anything that will potentially get them to a place they believe they need to escape.

What is the solution? How do we stop this?

I do not pretend to have all the answers; I am as faulty a mother as any other out there. I can only try my best, which I interpret as the following. Firstly, I try to educate my children in nutrition. I don't force them to finish their meals. I encourage them to eat vegetables by educating them on the benefits eating vegetables have to their bodies. Mostly it doesn't work, meaning that they can be incredibly headstrong, and nothing I say will convince them to eat what is on their plate if they don't want to. My attempts at educating them don't always change their mind about eating their food, but that doesn't make me stop educating them. I will continue to do it repeatedly because I hope that something I try to teach them sticks and that one day eating well will be a priority to them too, as they will know what they have to benefit from it.

I also do not encourage using food as a reward. When we have dessert on a particular day, they can still have dessert even if they had nothing of their main meal. But they cannot have three bowls of dessert, nor can they have something else to eat if they've refused to eat the meal that I prepared for them. I.e. I do not expect them to eat their food, that is their choice, but the next meal will only be when it is time for that next meal.

Regarding shame, when I see my children trying to hide something from me, I let them. It is so hard, one of the hardest things one can do. But I try to turn a blind eye. For example, if I see something they are trying to hide in their waste paper baskets on a Saturday morning while cleaning them out, I pretend I didn't see it. Or if my six-year-old has taken my makeup yet again, I will just put it back when I see it in her room and keep quiet. I do not want to start a fight over something minor. Instead, I wish to choose my battles.

Of course, I decide which battles to engage in, using my discretion, and if it were something serious, I would speak up. But if I can let it

slide, I do. I am not sure if this is the right way to go about things, but I wish my mum had waged fewer battles against me when I was still a child. Deciding to let small things slide is a decision I have made that had nothing with weight. When I was a pre-teen, I wanted to shave my legs badly. But my mum refused to buy me a razor. So I used hers. When she caught me, I felt so bad, but I didn't even get a chance to apologise. It turned into this massive fight that I still remember after all these years. It was then that I decided that I do not wish to make my children feel like that one day when they have done something they shouldn't have.

The most crucial thing regarding shame, I believe, is that I let my children see the imperfect me. Of course, I would love to be perfect and get everything right all the time. But that is unrealistic – not just for me, but for my children as well. I need them to see that I also make mistakes and what happens when I do. When I let rip a swear word, I say, "Oops! I am sorry. I should not have said that." I apologise to my children when I am wrong. I have even permitted my children to call me out on my bad behaviour. In the beginning, they were hesitant to do so, but now they do it quite comfortably. It helps. It opens my eyes to my flaws, and it allows them to identify harmful behaviour and makes them realise that I am also human. And 'just being human' does not make me wrong nor shameful.

The weight loss maze opened its arms to me and then imprisoned me when I was a young and ignorant child looking for some way to feel better about myself. I kept my love affair hidden – a secret. Food loved me, and I loved food in return. It was my only meaningful and loving relationship.

What I'd Like To Tell My Sister Now

Honestly, I feel like I have nothing that I wish to say to you. I want to set you free and let your spirit do whatever it is spirits do.

I think society over romanticises the female bond. There is this mother and daughter bond that is supposed to be unbreakable. Then, this sister bond is inseparable, joined at the hip, believing that we will be there for one another through thick and thin. I had mum, and I had you, but all I actually had were toxic relationships. There was nothing romantic about these relationships. They sucked me dry for the majority of the time. All these relationships had done was hurt me and leave me with emotionally empty voids yearning to be filled.

I never felt close to mum. But there were times in my life that I did feel close to you. Those were the last few years of my schooling career and the years after your initial clinic treatment up to about two years before your marriage.

So many days, I think about that morning before leaving for the university that you begged me not to leave you. It was still dark. I quickly popped into your room to say goodbye. We had a long road ahead of us and needed an early start. I had no idea what university and staying in residence would be like, nor did I know when I would see you again.

I expected you to be still asleep, but you were already awake — crying. You hardly ever cried. That morning might be the only time I remember you crying. I was usually the one in tears, the gloomy one. I even labelled myself as melancholy as I was always in tears. But, there you were crying, and I did not know what to make of it all. I didn't expect you to act that way, and I didn't know what to say when you asked me not to go.

You were seventeen; I was eighteen, and only then, for the first time, I realised that you did not want to be left alone with mum. How did you avoid it for so many years? Was I just always there?

I didn't understand your reaction to my leaving. In my mind, you were not affected in the same way that I was. You always made a beeline straight for your room whenever a fight started. I thought you were so clever. But you must've been listening? Were you scared? Or were you grateful that she wasn't fighting with you? When you begged me not to go, were you afraid that you were going to be at the receiving end of mum's temper with me not at home?

I couldn't stay even though you begged. I had to say no. You asked again. How could I remain? What was a possible reason for me not leaving as planned? It was unfair of you to ask. I needed to go. I had to go, and I just wanted to say goodbye. But it turned into a guilt trip that would haunt me for the rest of my life.

What happened after I left? I do not know. I do know that it could not have been easy for you. Every time I visited, you were less yourself and more absent in your communications with me. You crawled into a shell and refused to come out. I thought you were just a typical teenager.

You — headstrong and stubborn as always — refused to go to university on finishing school. I am sure that you wanted to go, but I also know that you could not secure a bursary. And for you, as it was for me, going into debt was a big no-no. You were even more anti-debt than I and so much more financially savvy than I ever was. You found a job and paid for online studies. I admired your tenacity.

I thought things were going well that first year and for a time after finishing school. I was wrong. I could see the rot clearly when dad passed away. You were not well and not coping. But I was studying, busy making a new life for myself. I was selfish. I should've been a better sister, made some plans.

I was surprised when you decided to move out of the house. Why would you struggle on your own, renting whatever room you could find when you could still stay at home at no cost? I now realise that the personal price of staying at home, at no cost, was far too high.

One day, mum called to let me know that you had tried to commit suicide. You found yourself admitted to a mental clinic. This attempt at taking your own life wasn't your first. I did not know what to make of it. The way mum handled the situation irritated me. It was so strange. I had the feeling that she was blaming me. She would also tell me not to talk about it to anyone else. Mum was ashamed of your sickness. She felt that you had disappointed her and expected me to be ashamed of you as well. The stigma around mental problems was alarmingly strong, and she passed that stigma down to me. I was upset with her and refused to listen to her lamentations. Instead, I asked my husband to visit you at the clinic — a peculiar visit — neither of us knew what to say to each other.

The way you decided to try and take your own life, I could not comprehend it. Why cut holes into your skin, mutilating yourself, and then injecting poison? How much must that have hurt? How did you even do it? Those marks remained — forever memories for you to see each day. That could never have been your intention. I am sure you wanted your suicide attempt to be successful. What did you think when you looked into the mirror? Did you see those marks and consider yourself victorious and rising out of your situation? Or did you consider yourself a failure when you could not take your own life? You always covered those marks — regardless of the weather — I assume you were ashamed of them.

The years passed, you graduated from university and completed a postgraduate degree. You became a certified accountant — working with money had always been your thing. You started your own business, and then you became an aunt. Mum passed away, you found love, and you married. I thought you were okay. I was blind. I am sorry that I was unable to see you.

I felt that you hated me. I am not sure what I did wrong or where I went wrong, but you hated me. You were the queen of one-sided conversations. Almost every message sent to you got a thumbs-up reply. You never tried to keep the conversation going unless you needed something, which wasn't often. You, like me, had a strong desire to be independent.

The most hurt I ever felt when you were still alive was on your wedding day. I was your bridesmaid, and I believe I was your bridesmaid purely because you wanted my children to be flower girls and pages. You did not want me there and made a point of excluding me. When it was time for you to get dressed, after an entire morning of doing make-up and hair, you ordered my eldest daughter and me to wait outside. You forbid us to walk to the ceremony area already — cause it would look suspicious if we were to be there before you.

We weren't allowed to see you in your dress or help you with your finishing touches. We were not allowed to drive with you to the ceremony area, and you had someone else signal at what stage we could start walking down. So we waited outside your room for what felt like hours. With nothing to do, already dressed and not allowed to go anywhere. I felt like you were sending a message to everyone, "This is my sister, and she is not important nor privileged enough to help me get dressed for my wedding. I do not even want her in my life." Why did you even invite me?

I've read so many times of suicide survivors having remorse. Their first thought when their feet left the platform to jump was "I don't want to jump. How do I fix this?" But that was never you. You wanted to be dead, and you tried again and again and again and again and again. Five suicide attempts! Ultimately you were successful. Your husband explained it so well. Others' mission each day was to stay alive, but yours was to stop yourself from killing yourself.

After you had taken your life, I had to sort through your earthly belongings. I come across little laminated notes where you instructed yourself not to be like me or listen to me. Those notes hurt! I tried so hard — too hard. The notes weren't even temporary post-it's; you went through all the trouble of printing them and having them laminated to put up all over your house and work area.

I also found self-help books on almost every topic you struggled with among your possessions, from falling pregnant to healing from toxic parent relationships. You wanted help, yet you didn't want to live? It is all so confusing.

Yes, I suppose I could sit here and write about all the could have's, should have's, and must have's, that maybe would have made things better. But what is the point? I did the best that I could and knew how. If I had to tell you something today, it would be that I should've acknowledged your hurt more. We should've recognised each other's hurt more. We should've communicated more and pretended less. I thought you were unaffected; you thought I had everything handed to me on a silver platter. Our assumptions cost us both dearly.

The Story Of Elna

The story of Elna is the story of answered prayers and how we are all merely instruments, humble servants. And that in order to serve, we have to be ourselves. Be a friend, listen, observe, tell a story, be present. We are all enough.

It is early Sunday morning. I am two months or so into therapy.

On Sunday mornings, we usually get our children in tow for the church service. Not today, though. The churches are still closed — no whining of not wanting to go to church today. Our church service will be happening online. Something is better than nothing, right?

I am so tired of my computer screen. Is this what human interaction has evolved to now? A face and a voice on the other side of an internet cable? Communication via a safe distance. Is this all we have left now? Something is better than nothing, right?

"Please, God, I do not want to go through this alone. I cannot. Please help me. How would I manage to go for an operation without my husband by my side? I cannot. I cannot go through this alone. I need Your help," I pray for the umpteenth time.

This Sunday morning, I am going for my Covid test. At least we can have elective procedures again. Something is better than nothing, right?

Pre-operation protocol dictates to expose your health to a queue of other potentially infected people. It makes no sense!

I question everything. Of the four people in the queue, who are the infected ones? Which one of you is going to make me sick? I do not want to be sick, but here are other living humans. I crave human interaction. I start talking to the woman in front of me; she doesn't look sick.

"Are you also here for a pre-op Covid test?" I ask, crossing my fingers.

"Yes, I am."

Phew! "Me as well. When will your operation be?"

"On Tuesday."

"Mine as well. What operation will you be having?"

I do not know how that was a fair question to ask a stranger; the question was out before I could stop myself. Nevertheless, she answers, "I am having endometriosis removed and am also having a scrape."

"O, a gynaecological procedure. I am also having a gynaecological operation, an ablation. Who is your gynaecologist?"

"Dr Viljoen."

"He is mine as well. Perhaps I will see you on Tuesday? The patients of one doctor are often placed together in the same ward, but I am not sure now with Covid," I say, drawing on some experience of having had previous operations. "What is your name?"

"I am Elna. And you are?"

"I am Mart-Mari. Nice to meet you, Elna. I will not forget your name. The name Elna is very special to me. It is the first letter of all four of my children's names in their birth order: Erik, Lia, Nardus and Adri."

"Nice to meet you too. Perhaps I will see you on Tuesday?" Elna says as the nurse calls her in.

On the Tuesday morning following my Covid test, my husband drops me off at the hospital reception. He is not allowed to walk in with me. I have to greet him in the parking lot and watch him drive away. I stand by myself in the hospital reception with my bag of essentials. Is this the last time that I'll see my husband?

Alone! I am alone and afraid. My prayer was not to be left here by myself. I am a strong independent woman, I tell myself. There is nothing that I cannot do if I apply myself entirely.

But that doesn't mean that I want to.

After being admitted, I walked the empty corridors to the ward where I was due for the day. I start unpacking my bag and settle into my situation.

I can do this, I am doing this, and I will rock this.

About half an hour later, Elna walks into the same ward. Her bed is diagonal across from mine. Minus husband herself, her situation is so similar to mine.

For the day, we become each other's family. We talk, share, exchange phone numbers and wish each other well on the way into the theatre. We complain when we are hungry, and we inquire when it takes a long time for the hospital to return our phones. I call the nurse when Elna starts bleeding post-surgery. We greet each other when it is time to go home.

I was not alone.

The following morning I lie in my bed when it suddenly dawns on me how my prayer was answered. The previous day I was too busy to realise it. At that moment, I felt incredibly loved. The feeling I experienced was better than all the somethings in the world combined. That feeling was not just better than nothing. That feeling is everything.

A Last Thought

> *"You can't go back and change the beginning but you can start where you are and change the ending."*
>
> — *C.S. Lewis*

I used the quote from C.S. Lewis above to conclude my very first open meeting talk. To me, it speaks of hope. Hope for a good ending and hope for a good life beyond that ending.

Something I'd come to realise, on all the journeys life has taken me, is that there is always an ending. A place where you need to compose yourself, find the new you and then be brave and vulnerable to start a new journey. I want to think of beginning everything to finish it ultimately. But sometimes, completing something is hard. It is hard to let go of something that you've perhaps learned to love. Sometimes it hurts to end something.

At the end of my weight loss journey, I found myself unsure how to start a new beginning from that point on forward. I also grieved the termination of my therapy journey, which was intensely personal, unsure how to pick myself up from that and go on with something new. Yet, in both of these cases, I figured out, by what I can only describe as grace, how to find that new me along with a new challenge and grow.

My maintenance journey has not ended yet. I don't believe there should be an end to my maintenance journey, as that will mean that I've stopped maintaining my weight loss. I do have this trait that makes me want to give up when life becomes complicated. I am aware of it now, and I can recognise it when I find myself at that mental stage. Yes, there will still be hard days ahead, but I genuinely believe that if I focus on living the healthiest, most active life that I can live, my weight should not be a problem to me ever again. I want to live a healthy and active life not because I see it as punishment but rather because I see myself showing myself some love. I can not make any promises, not even to myself. I can only try my best.

My writing journey has also not ended yet. I have found myself time and time again stuck in a hole while trying to finish this book, and even more so whenever someone would start editing it. This writing journey has been challenging as writing does not come naturally to me. Some people have a way with words; it is their talent. I feel what I do can best be described as verbal diarrhoea and a deep desire to get the text out of me. Yet, whenever I found myself stuck in one of my despair holes, I had my husband, friends, and page followers helping me out again. I had always thought that this book would be it, yet here I stand at the end of it, and I still desire to write! I want to continue improving my writing and maybe even one day publish another book. I wish to delve more into my mum and my sister's stories and the effects growing up in a perfect home, but that is rotten at the core has on people.

Considering the aforementioned idea, perhaps I have another memoir in me, or maybe I should instead look into writing erotica? The most fun chapter in this book for me to write was the erotic chapter. What can I say? I am a mum of four, who used to be eighty kilos overweight, who had been very happily married for almost seventeen years now, and I find myself enjoying writing erotica. What a confession that is to make!

I am not sure where life will take me, but I am looking forward to finding out. I want to embrace all the opportunities I can and live a wholesome and happy life.

After all is said and done, each morning, either my husband or I still weigh out twenty grams of cereal or raw oats and one-hundred-and-seventy grams of plain yoghurt for my breakfast. That is one complex carbohydrate portion and one dairy portion. Weighing out my breakfast is my humility anchor. I continued doing it throughout my Weigh-Less steps and after reaching goal weight. I do this to remind myself where I had come from and what I should be thankful for.

Continue following my journey at
www.facebook.com/martmarib

Acknowledgements

One big desire that I have in life is not to be needy. I want to be able to do everything on my own. Yet, losing eighty kilograms, working on myself and writing this book has taught me that I cannot do everything independently. Sometimes I have to swallow my pride and admit that I need help or accept any offered aid.

Here are the people without whom my journey could not have been possible.

Firstly I'd like to extend a big thank you to my therapist, Timothy Kieswetter.

* * *

Timothy, thank you for seeing that I needed help and offering to help. You have been the most amazing guide on this introspection journey of mine. I wish I could chat with you for one session each month forever and ever, but I also understand that that is not viable. The one quote from you that stands out to me is: "The only thing in life that you are responsible for is your poo. Nothing else is your responsibility to take on your shoulders." Maybe a bit extreme, but just what I need to remind myself of time and time again.

At one stage, your Whatsapp status read: "Sex therapist and stand-up comedian, but actually I just want to write." I never understood it before, but I do understand it now.

I cannot thank you enough for everything you've done for me. This book is the journal for your 'trophy case'.

* * *

In December 2020, I received a comment on my Emotional eating video shared with one of our local community groups. This comment was from Boo Prince. She asked if she could perhaps meet up with me.

Because I do not watch television or even listen to any radio, I had no idea who Boo was. I also often get requests from people who want to meet up, so it was not a strange request to me. I organised to meet up with her at a local restaurant. That day I met this wonderful new friend who wanted nothing more than to see me succeed and my story to reach as many people as possible. Boo is a voice and media coach, and she planted the seed in my head that became this book. If you have enjoyed my book, it is her whom you have to thank.

* * *

Boo, thank you! Thank you for believing in me, especially when I did not believe in myself. If it were not for you being the wonderful person that you are and guiding me, this book would've never happened.

* * *

One person I make not nearly enough mention of is my Weigh-Less group leader, Hannali Meyer. Hannali guided me for most of my weight loss journey and never doubted that I would lose all eighty kilograms. She even had custom made reward stickers printed for me. Weigh-Less has reward stickers for weight loss up to sixty kilograms. My children used to love it whenever I brought a new sticker home, and when I went over the sixty kilos lost mark, I feared they would become disappointed if I stopped receiving reward stickers. But Hannali made a plan. She used to keep my custom stickers pinned to my file, believing that I would earn them one day.

* * *

Hannali, you have been the most amazing friend and confidant. Thank you for never giving up on me. Thank you for all our chats and for being so proud of me. Your support had meant the world to me.

* * *

Someone very special to me is my friend, Hanneli Esterhuysen. For almost three years and over two continents, she graciously accepted my weekly weight updates. I could've never asked for a more supportive friend. When I started writing, she was always the first to read and comment on my work. Her enthusiastic voice notes were always the highlight of my day, and she pulled me out of so many of the holes I found myself in.

* * *

Hanneli, thank you for continuing to support me so selflessly. I don't think I would've even reached my goal weight if it wasn't for your support. Thank you for being my friend and remaining my friend even through your weight struggles.

* * *

To Jackie Ungerer, Hanneli Esterhuysen, Caroline Hirst, Tommy Diedericks, Fiona Hulme Brophy, Hanna Bresler, Tertia van der Merwe, Liesl Cronjé and Debbie Hishin who all either proofread, send comments back, talked through content with me for hours or helped with the editing of my first drafts. Thank you! Thank you for being my soundboard and sacrificing your opportunity to be surprised with what you read when the book is published.

And lastly, but definitely not least, I want to thank my husband, Derik. He gave me the space to write this book and has been the most supportive husband ever. I often needed to chat through ideas with someone, and he was always available and willing to listen — even in the middle of the night when certain pieces of text kept me awake.

* * *

Derik, thank you for being what I need — always! Thank you for putting up with all my moodiness and tantrums. Thank you for also showing me how to relax and let go. I love you more than I would ever be able to express in written words.

Eighty Kilos of Shame

Timeline

21 May 1981: I'm born.

2 December 1982: My sister is born.

1988: I start Grade One.

1989: My sister starts Grade One, and my older sister goes to university.

Middle 1997: I meet the man I would marry.
End 1997: I start my first diet.

11 February 1999: My husband and I start dating

2000: I start university.

28 April 2003: My dad passes away.

11 September 2004: I marry.

2 January 2008: My eldest is born.

February 2009: I join Weigh-Less for the first time.

26 April 2010: My second child is born.

Start of 2011: My hernia diagnosis.
11 November 2011: My third child is born.

2 September 2012: My mum passes away.

9 July 2014: My fourth child is born.

7 February 2017: I rejoin Weigh-Less.

17 April 2018: My hernia operation.
16 November 2018: My sister's suicide.

10 December 2019: I receive my goal weight certificate.

14 February 2020: My first ten-kilometre race.
28 March 2020: My first online video.
19 May 2020: My first therapy session.
14 July 2020: I start my Facebook page.

Resources

My Facebook page:
www.facebook.com/martmarib

Weigh-Less website:
www.weighless.org

My therapist, Timothy's website:
www.gesondeseks.co.za

My stylist friend, Marinda's Facebook page:
www.facebook.com/bibstyling

My Pilates instructor, Christiane's website:
christianeebert.com

My photographer friend, Jackie's website:
www.senzua.co.za

Printed in Great Britain
by Amazon